Hi
Gorgeous!
Starry Eyes and Toxic Lies

by
Melissa K. Dean

Edited by
Vivian A. Dean

Guinevere Press
Lakewood, Ohio

Published by Guinevere Press, P.O. Box 415, Lakewood, Ohio
44107

FIRST EDITION

ACKNOWLEDGEMENTS

I'm blessed by the support of many people who nurtured me during this project.

First and foremost, I thank my mother Vivian for her love and eye for detail. Thanks also to my father Gary, who helped Mom raise me with a role model for a healthy marriage.

Numerous hugs and kisses to my fiance Eric for his patience during the many evenings I sat before the computer. Most of all, his loving care helped renew my faith in romance.

Thanks to Leslie for supporting my goals and introducing me to her wonderful brother.

Hugs to my adoptive uncles Dale and Marty, who continue to provide non-judgmental support and good energy.

Hugs to Dan, my best friend from college whose love never wavered despite the distance placed between us by geography. Numerous circumstances in the last few years have prompted me to repeat the phrase we often said on the OU campus: What the f*ck? WTF indeed!

Thanks to employees at Lorain County Juvenile Court who privately supported my struggle against the establishment's hypocrisy.

Hugs also to various loved ones, colleagues, and acquaintances who expressed support in unique, and sometimes unrecognizable, ways.

I'd be remiss if I didn't express appreciation for companionship provided by furry felines. Poof, thanks for reminding me of bedtime. Burbles and Artemis... you're sorely missed, as is your dearly departed brother from Stark County.

I'm grateful for the written work of counselors like

Dr. Susan Forward and Patricia Evans, whose books helped nurture my journey towards emotional health.

Thanks to educators who nurtured me from kindergarten through law school. Special kudos to Michael Ventura, a teacher at Lancaster High School who encouraged me to question dogma and facts. Thanks also to Ohio University political science professor Dr. J. Frank Henderson for encouraging me to quit overanalyzing. "Melissa, just write!" Thanks, Professor Henderson. I did!

PREFACE

As I sat down last year to write this work , I recalled words from the Rolling Stone Magazine: What a long, strange trip it's been. Not only did a drive towards catharsis compel me to share that trip, but I realized that too many endured similar events through the world of on-line dating, many of which were longer, stranger, and far more abusive than mine. I could've healed behind closed doors, but their stories filled me with a desire to connect with survivors of similar madness. If I propel even *one* soul towards emotional health, my writing will be worth the effort.

In sharing my story, I've changed the names of most people I encountered along the way. This was done to protect the privacy of kind souls *and* lessen the power of unkind ones. It was also imperative to prevent reader distraction, for the aim of this work is to describe a journey rather than spotlight personalities. I leave it to those individuals to describe their own journeys.

Readers may note that I introduce each segment of my work with musical lyrics. I've always believed in the power of music to set a mood and speak to the human soul. Each lyrical segment speaks to the events and emotions I experienced on my journey. I share them as freely as the narrative that follows.

1. ANNA, BENAZIR, AND ME

I cannot put my finger on it now,
The child has grown, the dream is gone.
I have become comfortably numb.
- Pink Floyd, "Comfortably Numb"

Pop! *Cassidy, my fellow bartender, ducked as I plucked another champagne cork. We frantically prepared the bubbly as our New Year's Eve crowd trickled in the door. With only ten minutes to spare until 2008, we filled champagne glasses with the speed of lightning. Todd, our trusty disc jockey, approached the bar to ask if we were ready. "Sure," I said..."are you?"*

"You know it!" he said. "I'm even more ready for the New Year!" I asked the twenty-seven year old if he referred to his re-enlistment into the U.S. Army. "A new marriage... I've got a new baby... I'm gonna have a new career...health insurance for my family... it's gonna be a new life!"

How true, I thought. The turbulence of 2007 brought several beginnings and endings into my life. For the first time I felt genuine exuberance of the New Year, rather than pseudo-resolutions that littered the holiday. Only one year ago, I rang in the New Year with an empty bank account, a growing depression, and a failing marriage fraught with emotional abuse. Now I faced the world with a financial reserve of two months of living expenses, a happier outlook, a return to my authentic self, and a budding romance with an old friend- a true gentleman whose kindness and gentility renewed my faith in love. What a difference a year made!

"Ten..nine..," boomed Todd's voice over the sound system. "Eight...seven... six... five... four... three... two... one. Happy New Year!" Cassidy and I hugged. While 'Auld Lang Syne' still played, I grabbed

my cell phone and ran into the club's liquor room, where I called Eric. "Hi baby," I said.."I stole a few moments to call you." He sounded surprised..."That's so sweet of you, honey." Choking back tears, I explained that I wanted to let him know how important he was to me in the past year, and said, "I'm looking forward to spending the next year with you even more." He sounded moved. "I can't wait to see you after work!" he said.

2007 brought as many changes to my life as it did headlines to my television. Born during the Vietnam War, I grew up keenly aware of the world around me. The year's headlines saw the loss of two famous women whose lives eerily touched my own, albeit for drastically reasons: Vickie Lynn Marshall, a/k/a Anna Nicole Smith and former Pakistani prime minister Benazir Bhutto.

Despite being worlds apart from each other, these famous women met on the spiritual level of this lady lawyer in the American mid west. The little girl in me... the awkward teen that relished eye shadow and devoured CNN... always harbored a perfectionist desire to have Anna Nicole's looks **and** Bhutto's leadership skills. At seventeen, I was ill-prepared for the cultural barriers to integration of female brains and physical appeal, and woefully ignorant of dangers that lined the "beauty" and "brains" boxes of the Madonna/whore paradigm -- dangers that Anna & Benazir know all too well. Twenty years later I knew I possessed both attributes, but something was wrong. Anna and Benazir represented the duality of my nature, but the delicate balance between them had tilted dangerously in one direction. The former represented the woman I was becoming; the other represented the woman I was losing.

Despite divergent educational levels, numerous similarities existed between the former Playboy playmate and the Pakistani leader- at least, to the observant eye. To be sure, life wasn't a bowl of cherries for either woman- especially when it came to personal relationships. Their marriages drew accusations of financial shadiness that spawned public ridicule - Anna's marriage to millionaire J. Howard Marshall earned her a "golddigger" title, while Benazir's husband Asif Ali Zardari spent years in prison on corruption charges that brought down her second administration.

They died amidst blame games and controversy, simultaneously adored and despised by their nations. The women were blamed for their own downfall: Anna's drug abuse spawned indifference towards her death, while Pakistani President Pervez Musharraf snubbed Benazir: "For standing up outside the car, I think it was she to blame alone- nobody else. Responsibility is hers."[1]

Not quite a year before Cassidy and I served up the bubbly at a Cleveland night club, I lay on the living room floor of the apartment I shared with my husband Jack. As he busied himself at our computer, national news reported that former Playboy playmate and Trimspa spokes model Anna Nicole Smith died suddenly at the Seminole Hard Rock Hotel in Florida. The coroner's report later confirmed that a lethal drug cocktail, coupled with infection from injections of B-12 and human growth hormone, brought down the model. Documents from the medical examiner indicated that eight of the eleven drugs in her system were prescribed to Howard K. Stern,[2] her lawyer, manager, pseudo-husband, and enabler of her long-standing drug addiction.

A shadowy figure, Stern appeared in numerous interviews with Smith and abandoned his law practice in order to manage (i.e., make money from) her career. Although perceived by some to be Anna's puppy dog, unflattering posthumous details revealed his role in her poor emotional health. On October 20, 2007, Geraldo Rivera aired a disturbing video shot by Stern; it featured an incoherent Anna, stumbling around a pool in clown make-up, and passing off her bulging pregnant belly as mere "gas." Anna's behavior frightened the nine-year-old daughter of family friend Ford Shelly. Sadly, the girl is heard on the video begging Stern to call a doctor: "Howard, help!.. Cut the tape off and help her...I think we need the hospital." Stern, on the other hand, coos, "This is worth millions...this footage is worth money." [3] Despite Stern's weak allegation that Shelly "stole" the tape from his own family's house, he released the video to Fox News at no charge.

Staring at the ceiling, I pondered the parallels between my life and that of the model whose idolization of Marilyn Monroe eerily loomed over her death. The bombshell born Vickie Lynn Hogan and I were products of working class families. Our resumes were richly diverse. From food service to exotic dancing, we were determined to meet our respective goals- she wanted to raise her son, while I wanted to pass the bar exam. I wasn't a high school dropout like Anna, but our compulsive behaviors surrounding food and weight were strikingly similar: I shed fifty-five pounds from my 5'4" frame in 1999, while the buxom blonde reportedly lost sixty-nine pounds with the help of TrimSpa[4] and subsequently became its spokes model in a deal brokered by Howard K. Stern. We held strong political opinions that were overshadowed by sexualized images that took center stage: Anna's activism surrounding animal abuse and gay rights barely merited a footnote in her obituary, while my beliefs on law and government were squeezed into a paltry corner of the on-line universe called "Kitten's Korner."

More importantly, my life had taken recent turns with equally fatal ramifications. Three months prior to Anna Nicole's death, I reconciled with an emotionally abusive husband whose professional priority was to make money from my image, law degree, and any other talents he could exploit. During our marriage his only stint in gainful employment was cut short when the director of his radio station terminated his tenure as an advertising rep- with unemployment benefits. According to him, this generosity was accompanied by her encouragement to spend the following year building up our motorcycle cheesecake website, V-TwinGirls.com.

His boss' decision provided the ideal opportunity for Jack to cast me into the one-dimensional image of "Kitten" with ever-increasing intensity. Each unwholesome suggestion dripped onto my consciousness like water onto rock, slowly molding it. I convinced myself that my marital obligations included supporting this business that was "ours." Soon my focus included less law and social justice and more diuretics, fat burning pills, and restylane injections. Jack's efforts to alter my body were accompanied by efforts to alter my mood, including his encouragement for me to drink alcohol - a "lose-lose" proposition that included harsh criticism in the event I overindulged. I explored the possibility of the infamous B-12 shots that gave Anna her final infection. Although he never dared use the term "meal ticket" to describe me, I was repeatedly reminded that the fate of the V-TwinGirls rested on my ability to fulfill the sexy image of "Kitten" **and** manage financial matters. What began as a positive outlet to express my vivaciousness and balance my intellect became a futile exercise that endangered my physical and financial health. I was also living on borrowed time, for alcohol's high calories threatened his ideal of a thin Kitten. Anna's valium, ativan, and chloral hydrate were closer than I cared to admit.

My eyes traced the pattern in our ceiling as I listened to the grainy 9-1-1 tape: *"We need assistance to Room 607 at the Hard Rock. It's in reference to a white female. She's not breathing and not responsive.*

Actually, it's Anna Nicole Smith."[5]
       The blazing fireplace didn't quell my chill as I recalled a fall conversation with Jack. Driving home from a dance practice for the V-Twin Girls, his tirade about my rhythm skills turned into a morbid inspirational speech. "We (i.e., the business) need to get at least five more years out of you. You say you wanna go out on a high note while you're young? That's just a bullshit excuse. Look at Anna Nicole. She's what, thirty-eight, and **SHE** did it! So can you." The hair on the back of my neck stood up. I wanted more than five years....and I wanted more than my sedative-ridden corpse being wheeled out of a hospital beneath maroon velvet. One week following Anna's death, I left the household.
       Thousands of miles from the Texas town where Anna Nicole grew up, Benazir Bhutto was born into a prominent Shia Muslim family, the Pakistani equivalent to the American Kennedy dynasty. She began her college education in the United States, where she attended Radcliffe at Harvard University. Just as I fondly remember my philosophical explorations at Ohio University, she viewed her undergraduate education with nostalgia, calling it "four of the happiest years of my life" and saying that it "formed the very basis of [her] belief in democracy." We graduated cum laude in our respective classes, and continued our education at postgraduate levels- she at Oxford, and I at Cleveland-Marshall College of Law. We indulged our interest with the art of debate, for the exchange advanced public awareness on the key issues of our day.
       Benazir and I were on a mission- helping others...speaking for those with no voice. Although gender equality was important to us, sometimes we changed tactics: I learned that groups like the National Organization for Women didn't provide a vehicle for my larger vision, while Benazir realized that Muslim

extremism prevented her from instituting feminist reforms as quickly as she desired. Despite altering our methods, we remained opposed to the abuse of power- especially when it led to the injury of our loved ones. At seventeen, my awareness of child abuse was raised when my mother revealed troubling details of her childhood, thereby rendering me a life-long advocate for women and healthy families. Bhutto's activism was similarly accelerated when, scarcely two years out of college, her father was executed at the hands of Pakistan's military regime. After enduring an exile in the United Kingdom, she assumed her mother's position as leader of the Pakistani People's Party (PPP). Following the death of General Muhammad Zia-ul-Haq, her star rose during Pakistan's first open election in more than a decade. In November 1988, as I watched George Bush Sr. defeat Michael Dukakis for the American presidency, I also saw Bhutto become the first woman to head the government of a Muslim nation.

Indeed, Benazir and I found our political voice during the elections of 1988. Granted, our voice became less audible at various time periods, but it was never silenced. Law school, jobs, compulsive overeating, personal relationships, and a dysfunctional marriage occupied my attention over the years, while Bhutto was sidelined with a series of political pitfalls, losses, tragedies and exiles. In October 2007, after eight years in exile in Dubai and London, she risked everything to return to her original mission in her homeland. Although she survived a suicide bomb attack on her welcome caravan October 18, 2007, her luck ran out after a December campaign rally.

As I walked through my front door after returning from a holiday celebration with my parents, the gruesome footage greeted my eyes as CNN reported Bhutto's assassination. "No!" I exclaimed as my duffel bag hit the floor with a resounding thud. There was no way the political icon of my youth suffered the same fate as Anna Nicole Smith. For some reason I expected that Benazir would live as long as the idealism she symbolized. Out of sight, out of mind...her exile from the political scene and my exile from self-awareness let me take both of us for granted.

If Anna represented the woman in me that I was slowly becoming, and Benazir represented the woman I was losing, the message was clear. Regardless of my placement on the Anna-Benazir scale, I couldn't ignore either aspect of myself or exploit it on someone else's terms. Each end of the spectrum presented unique risks, especially in a culture saturated in the dual standards of the Madonna-whore complex. However, my three-year marriage witnessed repeated reminders that I faced *larger* risks while stationed in the spectrum's center. Like hermaphrodites, I possessed oppositional characteristics that rendered me a cultural oddity and the subject of exploitation- most notably, by the person closest to me. It was inevitable that I would eventually meet the ultimate fate of Anna and Benazir, but my legacy was hard to envision. Would I be remembered for walking a path of someone else's choosing and conforming to a pre-packaged box, or would I walk my own path of internal integration? My prim, intellectual "Madonna" side and adventurous appeal deserved equal respect. That respect had to begin with me.

"I haven't given myself away.
I belong to myself and always shall."
Benazir Bhutto (June 21, 1953 - December 27, 2007)

2. HI GORGEOUS

Every day is so wonderful
And suddenly, it's hard to breathe.
Now and then I get insecure
From all the pain; I'm so ashamed.
- Christina Aguilera, "Beautiful"

"Hi, gorgeous." I laughed out loud at his bold approach. One cold December night, I went to my computer desk and scanned the responses to my new profile on a singles website, match.com. Scarcely two days into my membership on the site, I was barraged with over thirty responses from Ohio gentlemen. Personal trainers, investment bankers, and postal carriers sent mild-mannered messages expressing interest in my profile, but this fellow cut right to the chase. Jack Cass, a retired Navy SEAL and divorced father of two with an interest in cooking and heavy metal, sliced through preliminaries with two simple words that captured my attention. Intrigued by his brazen method, I was amused at the idea that he thought my pictures were "gorgeous." As a woman who traditionally dissociated herself from the concept of physical appeal, I was flattered by his opinion. Just as psychologists often point out, my life-long efforts at distancing myself from "beautiful" category masked an equally strong fascination with it. One thing was certain, however: that fascination was spawned years before I responded to Jack's message.

Pssshht... I heard the chemical mist spew from Mom's hair spray can as I sat on my parents' bed in my family's Columbus, Ohio apartment. I covered my mouth unsuccessfully as I coughed from the chemical droplets that fell gently on the hardwood floor. Long before Anna Nicole Smith reached the public consciousness, my four-year-old eyes were fascinated by the cultural trappings of female beauty.... and the first glimpse I got came from my mother's regimen. It was intriguing and exciting to me- especially on Sundays, for that was the day I got to share her experience. Her brush moved at the speed of light through her brunette locks as she cast watchful glances at the clock. As the aerosol mist dissipated, I smelled the aroma of blueberry muffins rising from downstairs- a distinct sign that Dad was busy in the kitchen. My Sunday clothes spread on the bed, I watched her apply the minimalist makeup befitting a preacher's daughter. There was a sequence to this intricate exercise ...foundation, powder, blush, eye-liner, mascara...and a dab of Estee Lauder - or Flora Danica, perhaps- whatever fragrance struck her fancy. Then my chance came. I sat quietly as she picked up the curling iron and went to work, spraying my hair as I held my breath from the aerosol shower raining on my head. The ritual's glamour quickly faded as my legs were pushed into opaque leotards, or "toddler pantyhose." The fabric was similar to the day-long sermons that lay ahead- good for outer appearance, but asphyxiating.

The leotards, corduroy jumpers, frilly dresses, and patent leather shoes that lined my closet filled me with a sense of limitation. It didn't matter that other girls wore them. I longed for more. I idolized the trappings of my mother's beauty, even to the point of coveting her adult world of weight management, including Ayds diet candies. I was taught to read prior to kindergarten, so it was easy to discern the box that carried the mysterious candy, one of which I swiped. Barely tall enough to reach the counter top, I accomplished the stealthy exercise, only to gag on the cube of chocolate-flavored grit. I reasoned that if I could eat these morsels while small, I wouldn't have to worry about weight when I was Mommy's age. It was preventative weight care, with the convoluted wisdom of a four-year-old.

While mom was my first source of knowledge about female beauty, the rituals practiced by her sisters also captured my attention- most notably, the aunt for whom I was named: Melissa Kaye. She was, for the most part, an enigma to me. Like the character Colonel Nathan Jessup in the film "A Few Good Men," she was seldom seen, yet ever-present. Like Jessup's famous declaration, "You can't handle the truth!" she provided a tagline that set the backdrop and tone for my life. That tagline was her name. Our mannerisms, looks, compulsive-addictive tendencies, and even some of her romantic challenges resembled those faced by her namesake (e.g., Before finding happiness, she ended a marriage with a husband who wanted her to maintain a model-like standard of beauty). She was everything I was not: a sleek, mature fashion plate with a rebellious edge. Geographical distance coupled with a reluctance to embrace the Church of God, earned her the unofficial title of the family's black sheep, intensifying her allure in my eyes. Since her makeup was crafted with precision, it was sometimes a point of controversy to my highly-religious grandparents. I rarely had the opportunity to witness her cosmetic transformation like I did with Mom, but her striking brand of beauty was legendary in my mind.

Like many girls, I was plagued by a lack of confidence as my body blossomed, but my awkwardness exceeded the normal level of teenage angst. I lived with the pervasive belief that I did not measure up to the two women who shaped my concept of female beauty. It wasn't that I was never told by family members that I was cute or attractive, but these compliments never seeped into my consciousness. I freely accepted their praise for my intellect, an asset that left a trail of tangible evidence... honor roll certificates, plaques, and diplomas. Yet there was no such proof of my beauty, save for the loving words of family members whose objectivity I questioned.

Self-doubt followed me throughout junior high school, where I took solace in my identity as a nerd, indulging in over-sized tops and a sloppy appearance that masked my desire for affirmation. My gawky looks and crossword puzzles condemned me to an asexual teen existence sans male attention, so I cultivated the apathetic attitude for which my age group was famed. Neither straight A nor straight-out beautiful, I sought out friends that personified my position in no-student's-land: quirky, unassuming, outcasts. The closest was Kendra, a heavy-set girl with a red-headed mullet who portrayed her turbulent home life in the notes we passed back and forth between classes. Her gruff persona made her the perfect best friend for me- no discussion of icky feelings, just a sense of humor to deal with our world of teachers, algebra equations, book reports and lunchtime meanderings.

As Kendra and I strolled the halls of General Sherman Junior High School, aromas of French fries and Johnny marzetti wafted from cafeteria as the cooks prepped for lunch. I rarely looked forward to the mid-day break, for I had a love-hate relationship with food. Ten years after my Ayds diet candy caper, I graduated to the occasional theft of Mom's diet pills. My self-consciousness was multiplied by the fact that my styrofoam lunchbox was "different." I detached from the nourishment it symbolized, sometimes emptying its contents before my morning departure from the house. At fourteen, I was almost too embarrassed to be seen by peers eating at all. It was during this time I retired to the school restroom for my first (and only) experiment at purging the contents of my stomach. Thankfully I couldn't complete the act well.

Opportunities in academia and cosmetics arrived

with high school, I was allowed to create my own toy box of makeup like Mom and Aunt Kaye. As the sounds of Motley Crue and Tina Turner thundered through my boom box, I toyed with shades and colors that I imagined would transform me into a glamour queen. But I was still the proverbial nerd who sought out friends with like minds- including Kristen, a quiet unassuming honor student whose sarcastic wit and political philosophy bonded us as friends well after graduation. My senior year scrapbooks predicted my professional future. My classmates listed items like the senior prom under the year's "significant events, while my entry read, "Robert Bork nearly got on the Supreme Court." Except for Kristen, I didn't know many teens whose brow furrowed as they watched this bearded gent justify to the Senate why judges that applied the Constitution to *all* Americans "legislated from the bench," while conservative judges who produced exclusionary results were reasonable. I could spot flawed legal reasoning like cheap cosmetics, and I was one of the few seniors paying rapt attention to the high stakes game on the Senate floor.

As I focused on the political world that Benazir Bhutto called home, the dual-sided coin of eating dysfunction flipped from undereating to gorging on various comfort foods. Chocolate chip cookies, macaroni & cheese, and late night burger binges with my family became the solace for my restless dissatisfaction. Youth saved me from a thickening waistline, but it was a brief reprieve. Amazingly I danced my prom night away in a size five gown. Two academic degrees and numerous political marches later, I found myself shopping for jeans at Lane Bryant. As I took a size sixteen petite to the register, I reached into my pocket for pack of Velamints. Depressed over my first failed attempt at the bar exam, I reached a point where I had to maintain an edible substance within easy reach. That day I wrote *much* more than the words "Lane Bryant" in my checkbook- I wrote my own reality check that catapulted me into the rooms of Overeaters Anonymous, where I learned the principles that assisted me in sliding into a size four.

"Will there be anything else for you today?" the Rubenesque clerk asked me.

"Yeah," I thought, "..a magic pill to take so that I never have to shop here again."

To a normal eater, the solution seemed simple. If I didn't want to be fat and unhappy with myself, all I needed to do was stop stuffing my face. But to an addictive eater like me, the laws of cause and effect were meaningless. I was not unlike compulsive gamblers and drug addicts. Tearing me away from the Cinnabon counter was like tearing an alcoholic away from the bar at closing time, and it wasn't uncommon for me to stop by Pizza Hut for a standard dinner- a medium pan pizza.

In addition to feeling ugly, two failed attempts at the Ohio bar examination left me feeling extraordinarily stupid and financially broke. My inability to obtain a job as an attorney, coupled with increasing debt and student loans, added up to seven- Chapter 7, that is. At twenty-eight I made the gut-wrenching decision to file for bankruptcy. With bills and tax returns in hand, I trudged to the office of my friend Ernie, a part-time prosecutor. Like a kindly uncle, he guided me through the process that I kept a secret from family and (most) friends. As I sat before the bankruptcy trustee, a feeling flooded over me that I hadn't felt since I bought those size sixteens from Lane Bryant. It was shame, mixed with a firm resolve to never find myself in that situation again. Somehow, I would find the money necessary to purchase a prep course for the bar exam, become an attorney, and make enough money to pay my bills.

My wheels turned furiously as I thought of ways to raise the money for the prep course... paying off a few old debts owed to friends would be a bonus. Retail stores and restaurants offered long hours and little pay. Then it happened. As I perused the help wanted section in Cleveland's Free Times magazine, one ad in particular stood out. Amber Lounge, a local gentleman's club, was "now hiring entertainers." No experience was necessary. At a size 8, I was midway through my weight loss and still plagued with self-doubt: I was too fat, my breasts were too small, and I was brunette. I was far from the big-chested blonde bombshell I fancied the typical stripper to be.

I tossed those negative thoughts aside as I delved into the mythical make-up toy box of Mom and Aunt Kay to create the most beautiful woman possible-or, at least, a woman that could appeal to the club's clientele. The dark shades and dramatic brush strokes were a refreshing change from the understated look I wore to court. I was preparing to enter a new phase of the Benazir-Anna continuum, and no simple black eyeliner would do. I took one last look in my duffel bag: High heels.. white bra and hot pants.. white mini-dress.. burgundy lipstick. Off I went.

I opened the door, which featured a big white sign that read, "Must be over 21 to enter." A broad-shouldered man greeted me from a security window. "Can I help you?"

"I'm here to speak with someone about auditioning to be a dancer." The buzzer sounded as I heard him say, "Come on in." Stale smoke billowed out of the door as my eyes struggled to adjust to the darkness. He directed me to have a seat near the bar until the manager was ready to see me. I made small talk with the waitress while sizing up my surroundings. Once she realized this was my first dancing audition, she began a pep talk. "Don't worry... just watch a few of the girls and you'll see how it's done."

As the DJ announced the next dancer, I heard the metallic introduction to Alice Cooper's song "Poison." I saw a statuesque woman in a red sparkly mini-dress strolling towards the brass pole, her ample hips swaying as she neared it. Her long straight brown hair flew as she twirled around effortlessly. Neither blond nor rail-thin, she was the embodiment of sultry beauty. Grasping the pole, she stared straight ahead, her brown eyes vacant with exhaustion. "You picked a good time to come in," the waitress exclaimed, "it's shift change." I barely heard her, still mesmerized by the dancer's look. Although her face was void of expression, her ruby lips finally cracked a smile as she leaned down to accept tips from several customers. Suddenly I felt out of my league.

The manager emerged from a door behind the bar, and the bartender signaled me to his office. A portly dark-skinned man with silver hair motioned me to sit. "I am Nani, the manager," he said with a thick Indian accent. He scanned my application as he peered over his glasses at me, explaining the mechanics of table dances, tips, and dancer outfits: "You cane wayr a bee-kee-nee....a mee-nee skart..see-thru and maysh are good, velly velly good." I nodded.

"What stage name will you use?" Caught off guard, I stammered, "Brandy." Moments later, Nani escorted me to the dressing room, where the deadly combination of floral body splash and smoke assaulted my senses. Women of every ethnicity and hair color tumbled on top of each other in a frantic search for clothing space. The bright light wasn't kind to the bevy of feminine bodies sliding into snug costumes, for every dimple of cellulite.. every scar.. every stretch mark.. was accentuated in the crowded room. "Anyone got any Dermablend?" someone shouted. Train cases and cosmetic pouches lined the counter top as mirror space became a prized commodity in this cubbyhole I later dubbed "the great equalizer." I dressed and sped to the DJ booth. Turning from the security window, the broad gent introduced himself. "I'm Bill. I'm the DJ here. I help with security too. What music do you like?" My taste for 80's dance and rock seemed no problem for Bill, who searched his musical library. "You'll be next. During the first song, you'll keep everything on, second song is topless," he said.

I leaned against the wall near the stage, where I watched the dancers emerge from the dressing room and awaited my cue. The women I'd just seen bore little resemblance to the goddesses on stilettos that strode confidently out of "the equalizer." Years after watching Mom and Aunt Kaye's cosmetic transformations, I was no less fascinated by female beauty now than I was at five. Although it was apparent that women of different looks - even sizes- could perform in this profession, I remained cynical about my appeal. Staring at my white garter, I pondered the irony of a feminist venturing into Anna Nicole's territory. It seemed a long way from the halls of justice through which I'd walked only hours earlier. But I was there for a reason, and I intended to keep my goal in mind. Someday I would turn this into an experience that transcended the brass pole.   Suddenly Bill's voice thundered, "And now... making her debut at Amber's Cabaret... the lovely Miss Brandy." As I made my way to the stage, the opening riff of The Tubes' dance classic "She's A Beauty" filled the club. Never before was I so consciously aware of eyes watching me. As I sashayed down the stage, my mind flipped through all the flash cards of information on public performance I learned in debate and drama classes: Make eye contact, smile, use as much stage space as possible- and stay balanced on platform heels! I learned not to dance faster than my normal range of motion. It became apparent that intricate pole tricks were out of the question for me, but it became *equally* apparent that acrobatics were not an integral part of financial success. Rather, it was confidence and interpersonal skills- i.e., the art of flirting- that bore the key. Therein lay the challenge for a woman with a life-long tendency to doubt her attractiveness. Not only did I have to believe in my own appeal (or at least pretend I did), but my earnings depended upon my ability to read the nonverbal cues of clientele who found me attractive. Each glance, smile, nod, or head turn could mean anywhere from $20 to $200. It wasn't the act of disrobing itself, but this particular aspect of the business that presented my biggest hurdle. It wasn't until the third week that I perfected the requisite façade of self-confidence to earn a reasonable income.

I spent the next few months witnessing the destruction of numerous myths surrounding the exotic dancing industry, many of which I believed at one time. The substance-addicted stripper of legend was no less common than the cocaine addicts working behind the bar or the alcoholic lawyers and judges I met outside the clubs. However, the stripper gained more notoriety for addiction than members of nonsexual male-dominated professions. I also encountered the specter of rape and sexual abuse that overshadowed the industry, for I'd always been taught that most dancers were abuse survivors working out old issues. While I was saddened by the experiences of entertainers who had been traumatized in their lives, I realized their stories were equally common among members of other female-dominated professions- e.g., nursing. These stereotypes shrank as my bank account grew. Within a couple months I plunked down $550 dollars for a bar exam prep course and paid off some bills. With my goal met, I exchanged my garter for a briefcase.

Persistence paid off when I learned in November of 1999 that I finally passed the mother of all tests. After several months of maintaining a solo law practice while working two part-time jobs, the juvenile court hired me as a magistrate for their intake department. With a resume of serving women and families, I was a shoe-in for the position that led me back into Benazir Bhutto's territory of advocacy. I was welcomed by my fellow magistrates in the all-female intake department, and befriended many of the staff at the youth detention facilities- including JC, a fifty-ish Vietnam vet with a West Virginian drawl. Two months into my tenure at the court, I sat in my office on a chilly fall evening, pouring over the case file of a juvenile whose parents had reported their son for unruly behavior. As I hung up the phone with the youth's mother, a dark-haired young gentleman walked thru the hall shaking a plastic bottle in his right hand. He peered into my office. I looked up.

"Hi," he said, extending his arm. "I'm Ed. Ed Bergman. I work in the back, in the boys' detention home. I work night shift, but they called me in early today. Nice to meet you... you must be the new magistrate."

"Yes," I said, shaking his hand. "Nice to meet you too. Overtime makes you thirsty, eh?"

"Oh, this," he shrugged, glancing down at the bottle. "It's a protein shake. The guys in the back always order pizza... this is better." His broad build revealed his health-consciousness, which became one of the topics we chatted about during the next half hour. In addition to working full-time, he said, he was working on his masters degree. He looked at his watch..."Whoa, I better get back. They're probably wondering where I am." It was ten minutes past my quitting time.

"Have a good night," I said. "Don't let those kids wear you out."

Months later JC clued me in that the lad held an interest that was more than platonic. "No way," I told him.

"Yes, way!" he exclaimed. "Can't you tell?"

"Well, I see him sometimes at the gym too... I just don't get that impression," I said as JC rolled his eyes. "Besides," I explained, "I have a boyfriend and I'm pretty happy right now."

"That's fine, dear. I'm happy for you...I'm just sayin' the interest is there, that's all."

Despite JC's words, I couldn't bring myself to believe that the gentleman was interested. Despite my experience in the exotic dancing industry, I still found it difficult to believe that someone else considered me attractive. Absent displays of interest that were characteristic of that highly-charged environment, I was adrift in a sea of male-female communication without cues.

Over a year following JC's eye-rolling, I prepared for my first vacation in several years- a New Age health and wellness retreat in Gulf Shores, Alabama. I scoured my Elyria apartment for the papers from retreat organizers, only to realize I'd left them at work. Frantically, I called the detention home and informed the night control room clerk that I would shortly be entering the building to retrieve some items from my office. "No problem, ma'am," he said.

Cursing my forgetfulness, I rolled into the parking lot and approached the building. "Front doors, please." I said into the speaker.

I rummaged through my file drawer. As I stapled my papers together, I heard the click of "Door 11," the entryway into the detention facility. A familiar face appeared. It was Ed.

"Hello there," he said. "Thought I'd come back and say hi."

"I had to get some of my vacation materials," I explained.

"Going anywhere fun?" he asked.

Once again, we spent the next half hour small talking on a variety of topics, ranging from vacation to politics. I noticed the time. "Oops, I better let you get back to work," I laughed.

He shrugged, "They don't care. It's dead back there. We only had one intake tonight."

As we exited, he extended his hand, as if to shake my mine- an odd gesture, since we were saying goodbye rather than greeting. Nevertheless, I reached out in reciprocation.

"It was nice seeing you again," he said, still holding my hand. "Hopefully I'll see you before you leave, but if I don't, have a good vacation!"

"Thanks," I said. "Make sure those kids back there behave."

"I'll try... that's a tall order. Take care now."

He smiled as we paused briefly in awkward silence, then dropped our hands.

It wasn't until I walked to my car that I finally realized that JC was right. I looked at my right hand. Now it seemed obvious. "Weird," I thought. But what to do about it? Ed seemed a nice fellow. The professional in me thought it unwise to pursue a romantic interest with a colleague, but I also knew we weren't in the same department. I decided to leave it up the universe to present an opportunity.

An apparent opportunity arrived several weeks after I returned from the South. As I entered my gym, I passed by the weight room on my way upstairs. There he was. He looked and waved. I headed upstairs to find that he'd followed me. Several minutes of small talk later, I took the plunge and invited him to coffee.

"Sounds great," he said.

"Give me a call if you wanna grab some java. You have my office number, and you guys at the DH have my home number too. Just give me a shout whenever."

"Great," he smiled, as he touched my shoulder. "You have a good one."

Days turned into weeks. No phone call came. Perhaps I'd been wrong. How could I have been that dumb to read so much into trivial gestures? I shrugged off my misstep and pledged to avoid the same mistake unless I was certain of someone's interest. But how could I ever be certain, except when I waited for the other person's invitation? A lifetime of passivity was unacceptable. But there was an idea I hadn't yet explored: on-line dating. Match.com beckoned, and I answered its call. My profile garnered instant responses, including the one that would alter my life for several years to come.

"Hi gorgeous!" Obvious. Bold. Hard to mistake.

3. THE SALES PITCH

Who are you.... who, who
I really wanna know.... who, who
Tell me, who are you.... who, who
'Cause I really wanna know.... who, who.
- The Who, "Who Are You?"

Those wintry days were warmed by my
excitement each time I checked my e-mail for a message
from Jack. "Hi gorgeous" got his foot in my door, but he
needed to do more. Seduction is seldom accomplished
by denigrating insults. Those techniques would have to
wait until he secured my commitment, and that was
months away. Attracting me was no small feat given that
he touted membership in the United States military's most
elite killing forces. I associated Navy SEALS, Rangers,
Deltas and Green Berets with the same machismo that
repulsed me since birth. Despite my preconceptions
about these men, this particular "SEAL" won me over with
an arsenal containing more firepower than the entire US
Armed Forces: charm and culinary expertise.

As days passed, our internet chats spawned
exchanges about television, politics, the humor of South
Park, and the vocals of Rob Zombie. Within days we
moved from the keyboard to the phone. My new love
interest was entranced by not only my looks, he said...
but my intellect, especially the unpretentious way I
approached the legal profession and my desire to help
others. Little did I know, but this aspect of my
professional life revealed the caring heart and empathic
nature that rendered me a perfect victim for a exploitive
predator. The fact I was reading a book on the exotic
dancing industry bore a titillating possibility of my former
affiliation with it, which enhanced his fascination. I, on the
other hand, was mesmerized by his throaty voice, eyes,

self-assuredness and passion. His self-employment as a public speaker and salesman of outdoor supplies gave him freedom in his schedule for lunch. "You name the day," he declared.

We bridged our geographical distance halfway. As I walked in the door of the Winking Lizard Tavern, out of the left corner of my eye I saw Jack. We smiled in mutual recognition as our eyes met, and we shook hands. Conversation superseded our interest in salads as we prattled on about various topics, including the characteristics we valued and disliked in potential mates. He spurned spoiled princesses and victim-oriented women, a group that included his mom- a counselor "ahead of her time", yet victimized by his Baptist father's verbal abuse and infidelity with Jack's piano teacher. He hated civilians, abhorred dishonesty, and disloyalty-especially infidelity.

My bleeding heart was moved by his tale of woe, which he fully anticipated. Here was a man who'd been wounded on the battlefields of war and romance. "I let women walk all over me," he proclaimed. The three purple hearts to which he laid claim paled in comparison to the heart he said was repeatedly broken by women who'd either cheated or bilked him out of money. "Learning to trust is a difficult task for me," he said.

It was shattered first by long-term girlfriend Dina, whose cheating ways became the talk of the town while he sent all his military paychecks home to her. He described their first meeting at the annual Saint Clement's Festival. Their teen affair blossomed, and young lust led to the inevitable. At seventeen, he became a father. His father pressured him to join the military, an action that Jack acknowledged bestowed upon him the necessary structure to support his new family. With the help of a military sponsored loan, his father assisted Dina in building the house in which he remained for years. He recounted numerous tales of arriving home on military leave to find her entangled in sexual misdeeds. Her exploits caused him to doubt the paternity of his eldest son, Jack Jr. "I don't know if he's mine," Jack declared, "but it doesn't matter now. I love him just the same." His determination led him into the civilian workforce, where he got a job working for the railroad, a position that returned him to the role of absent father and betrayed boyfriend. Several affairs and one son later, the two parted company as Dina left the boys with Jack.

Alas, Jack said his heart was broken again, this time by ex-wife Theresa. He met the petite blonde at the community college, where he took classes to obtain a real estate license. Although he never furthered that career, the two dated as he worked for the railroad. Eventually, he said, he was faced with a choice- marry Theresa or the eighteen-year-old babysitter whose admiration captured his fancy. He finally resolved the quandary upon concluding that he needed Theresa's assistance with raising his sons. "She was good for the kids," he explained.

Jack's continual absence took its toll as Theresa tired of his military and civilian careers. "She hated the military, and what it did to the boys to see me in the hospital with combat wounds," he said, shaking his head. "I gave it up to save our marriage," an effort that bore little fruit. Neither defense contracting nor professional fishing brought the lifestyle he valiantly tried to provide her, the boys, and the two children they brought into the world. Meanwhile, postpartum depression allegedly reared its head following the arrival of their daughter Jill. He generously attempted to replenish her depleted esteem by purchasing her a breast augmentation. Scarcely three months following her operation, he said, she left him suddenly while he was out of town on business.

"I want a divorce," said the flat voice at the other end of his cell phone, as he recalled pulling over to the side of the road in shock. He returned to Ohio only to find his house empty, save for his second eldest son Jay. While future conversations yielded allegations of Theresa's infidelity, he stopped in mid-sentence that day. "Enough about her. I don't want to dishearten you today; I want to get to know you," he said.

Our philosophy towards financial status was similar. "I'm not a rich man," he explained as he described the rigorous upkeep required at his rural Stark County home. He leaned inward with keen interest as I described my distaste for high-powered law firms, affinity with pagan spirituality, and desire for a sensitive gentleman in my life. "You've never had a man sensitized by combat," he proclaimed as he looked straight into my eyes. He seemed especially curious about the book I was reading on exotic dancing..."I gotta ask, have you ever stripped?" I volunteered how my brief stint in the industry had funded my bar exam, and that I felt richer for the experience. Unfazed, he replied, "No worries. It seems like I've always dated either current, or former, strippers."

"Really?" I asked, "Is your ex-wife a former dancer?"

"Oh no," he said, "but I dated a couple of them after we split." He described how his range of personal acquaintances widened during his brief tenure as security for Gatsby's Pub, a Canton strip club that provided a professional outlet following his return from a mission in Afghanistan. "It was a tough time financially," he admitted.

"Everyone on Team One got activated after 9/11," he said, his voice lowering with an air of mystery. "I can't tell you specifics on my mission, but it was hard coming back to the states. I didn't have any speeches booked at outdoors shows. Companies didn't want to hire me, 'cause I could be called back at any moment. But I was good at hand-to-hand combat. Gatsby's needed someone like me to bounce for them, so I did. No matter what, I've always supported my kids." Although he enjoyed life, he prided himself on fulfilling his obligations: "I'm twelve years old, with responsibility," he said with a mischievous smile.

The moment arrived when our lunch had to end. My retail shift at the local mall beckoned.

"May I have a box for this?" he asked the waitress, pointing towards his half-eaten salad. He explained, "I have an aunt that lives down the street. She's elderly and doesn't cook for herself. I'm gonna run this over... gives me an excuse to check on her." In the coming days, I could think of nothing else except Jack as I rode the pink cloud of love. We meshed so well that it seemed karmic. And karmic it was- although not for the reason I thought.

An observant psychologist could have analyzed that lunch conversation and explained that Jack unknowingly revealed noteworthy info. His mom's victimization by dad, coupled with alleged infidelity of several mates, didn't add up to a recipe of respect for women- his fawning compliments to me notwithstanding..."Have you ever modeled? You should consider it." The only categories of women in his life were victims, unfaithful sluts, and strippers. Despite obligatory secretiveness on classified details, Jack's braggadocio regarding military assignments pointed to aggression, a fact I was willing to overlook in the name of open-mindedness. I couldn't judge all military men as violent, could I? His declaration of not being rich, and his ability to meet for lunch almost any day signaled the possibility of financial instability, but I wasn't paying attention. I was too busy viewing him through glasses rosier than my chilly cheeks on Christmas Day.

       Holiday cheer and newfound love filled me with excitement as I prepared to visit my parents on Christmas Eve. My cats watched quizzically as I filled their dishes and packed up my car. I scribbled a note for their sitter, donned my Santa cap with leopard print trim, and off I went for my three-hour sojourn to Lancaster, Ohio. Years of holiday commercialism hadn't dampened my festive nature, for no amount of gifts surpassed the warmth I associated with the love of my family at that time. As I unlocked the door, familiar aromas of potpourri and baked goods greeted me as my parents' three feline friends milled around my feet. Mom hugged me, then Dad. I didn't realize that would be the last time I experienced holiday warmth for four years.

       After Christmas, I asked Jack if he wanted to spend New Year's Eve together, to which he enthusiastically agreed. I invited him to the annual midnight cruise on the Cleveland-based Nautica Queen. After he accepted, I purchased tickets. Excitement filled the air as he drove us to Cleveland in his diesel-powered van, while the goth sounds of Type O Negative and A Perfect Circle decorated the night. With he in his suit and I in my blue sparkle gown, we feasted on fine cuisine, sipped champagne and danced the night away to 2004. As we chatted with several couples, I asked one woman to take several pictures of us- one of which later produced an instinctive response from my mother, who sensed danger. Although Jack accepted my invitation to come inside my apartment, he cut his visit short. He expressed guilt that his family dog Minnie remained confined in the house. "If I don't let her out soon, I'll find a mess on the rug," he laughed.

       While it was true that poor Minnie beckoned, she wasn't the only female that drew him back to Massillon at 2:30am. Jack's steady girlfriend of two years, known to me only as his "platonic" friend Linda, awaited his return that evening. She was equally ignorant of his whereabouts as I was to her existence- at least, until her later discovery of our Nautica Queen tickets in his suit pocket revealed the ruse. It was not the first lie revealed to her, and it would certainly not be the last for either of us.

As Jack's relationship with Linda continued, the stars in my eyes grew with intensity- a phenomenon that was quite apparent to my colleagues at juvenile court. "Well now!" exclaimed my fellow magistrate Joanne, as she eyed my spaghetti-strapped arms embracing Jack in our New Year's photos. News of my courtship reached the control room at the boys' detention facility, where JC voiced cautious support. As Christmas trees faded into Valentine hearts, Jack announced one February day that he was planning a Valentine trip. "I'm not going to tell you where yet, but it will only be for the weekend. Plan ahead for your cats." Days later he revealed our destination: Niagara Falls. JC had one thing to say about Jack's surprise: "Hmm..." He busied himself with the levers on the control panel. When I inquired beyond his monosyllabic response, he said, "No darlin', it sounds great....but things have a way of happening in Niagara Falls, ya know? Just be careful." No problem, I assured him. I proposed that all of us get together at a local watering hole. I explained it would the perfect opportunity for Jack and the guys at the detention home to meet each other. "Cool," he said, "I'll talk to the guys. We can go out after y'all return from Niagara."

Friday afternoon, Jack appeared at my door with Valentine's Day card in hand and a passionate kiss on his lips. I handed him the gift bag of Valentine goodies I'd purchased- including a Mushroomhead tee from Hot Topic. "Sorry I'm late," he said. "I had to borrow my dad's car. Didn't think my old van would get us to Niagara and back." I didn't think to consider why he was taking a trip to Niagara Falls when he couldn't afford a good vehicle. I asked about his animals. He assured me that his pal Linda was taking care of them. "I got a friend who looks in on them for me a lot when I'm away. They'll be fine." Off we went to the land of waterfalls, stopping at places like the Hard Rock Café. During that weekend, discussed his solitary lifestyle. "I hate people," he proclaimed as he explained that the majority of his buddies were among the combat-dead.

"You know," he paused thoughtfully, as his hands slid gently down the steering wheel. "I hope it doesn't bother you when I talk about my military past. I don't like to talk about it too much, but I also want to let you understand me better. Sometimes it even makes *me* uncomfortable. I'd just hate to alienate you." I assured him that he needn't worry. I viewed his combat experiences as traumatic events, so I let him initiate those discussions. Indeed he initiated those talks, and repeatedly so. Post-Niagara dates reflected a continual return to combat-oriented discussions, a tendency not often seen in those involved in special operations warfare, for military protocol requires discretion regarding such matters. However, my civilian life had not endowed me with the awareness necessary to spot this inconsistency. Yet still the red flag waved, as I was the audience for numerous cathartic narratives riddled with references to fallen comrades.

With his mother and nearly all his SEAL team members dead, he lacked a solid base of support, he explained. His two sisters lived out of town, and his father's abrasive attitude rendered him emotionally unavailable. Aside from his elderly Aunt Glenda, one bright spot remained, however dysfunctional it seemed: His civilian pal Linda, a divorcee whose helpful tendencies he appreciated, but whose feelings exceeded platonic friendship. "Don't get me wrong, she's a great friend. She helps me in the yard, goes bike-riding, she's even loaned me some money in hard times. She just wants to be more than friends," he said, shaking his head. "I've told her where I stand, and she says she's fine with that but... she wants more."

He described how their shared experience as divorced parents made them a special tag team. "We help each other out with our kids," he said as he explained how Linda often babysat his children, while he served as a father figure to her teenage daughter. Since she was a viable part of Jack's life, I proposed a double date to diffuse tension and clarify boundaries. "Oh, she's too insecure....she'd never do it," he scoffed. "I'm just not meant to have many friends, I guess."

The fantasy of Niagara Falls dissolved into Ohio reality as Jack dropped me off at my apartment before returning to Massillon. Our return brought the task of sharing our romance to loved ones. As my co-workers planned an outing, Jack and I prepared for family introductions. He stressed the significance of this step as he explained that I was the only woman he'd brought around his kids in several months. "Why don't you come to the house next week when the kids are over?" he asked. "I'll cook some dinner, and you can meet each other. It will be a comfortable environment." Due to wintry weather, I arrived forty-five minutes late. "I hope you don't mind. They're used to eating by a certain time, and it got to be late. I didn't know if you were coming."

Peering into the darkened den, I saw two small blond figures laying in front of a television. As Jack introduced me to seven-year-old Jill and twelve-year-old Jason, who nodded a brief "hey." Their eyes remained glued to the screen. He shrugged. "They're entranced with their tv shows. C'mon..you must be hungry." He led me to the dining room table, as he busied himself in the kitchen. "It's nothing fancy. Hope you don't mind spaghetti," as I heard the clanking of silverware against a plate. After serving me at the dining room table, he thanked me for coming. "Of couse," I said, as I bemoaned the weather's theft of quality time with the kids. Seeing that he didn't have a plate in front of him, I asked if he was hungry. "Nah, I'm fine," he said, "I ate pasta with the kids." Following my repast, we went into the den and sat on the sofa.

During a commercial, Jack tried to engage the kids in conversation with me, with minimal success. I didn't force them into an unwanted interaction, but instead let them guide our small talk. After he sent them to bed, I headed off in the wintry weather back to Elyria.

My eyes bleary from four hours of sleep, I headed to work the following morning. Following afternoon hearings, I paid JC a visit. "I talked with some of the guys," he said. "They're game...Saturday ok?" We settled on a local pub. Although my fellow magistrates bowed out of the outing, most of the fellows at the detention home were happy for an opportunity to drink and laugh.

"You're excited about this, aren't you?" Jack asked after he arrived at my door. I nodded.

"You have a lot in common with JC," I said. "We're gonna have a great time."

Moments later, he posed an odd question. "Did you tell him I was in the Navy?" he asked.

"Sure," I said, "...it's part of a commonality. Was that okay?" I fretted that I'd done something wrong. I shared Jack's pride in his service.

"Oh, it's not a problem," he assured. "Did you tell him I was a SEAL?"

"No; I figured I'd leave that up to you."

"Good."

I needn't have worried. After hands were shaken

and beer flowed like water, Jack volunteered his service in the Navy. Laughter dominated our table as JC and Jack exchanged war stories. Jack launched into his SEAL exploits while my buddy maintained a respectful distance from his tales of special warfare. "Yeah I knew some of those guys in the Navy. When we saw the trident, we knew not to ask…and they didn't tell." The time for goodbyes came quickly.

The night silence was only broken by the whir of the car engine as we rolled down the highway. "They're a nice bunch of guys," Jack said. "Do you think JC liked me?"

"I'm sure he did."

After Monday's hearings I strolled into the control room. "So," I asked JC, "did you have a nice time Saturday?"

"I sure did. Jack seems like a nice guy. He's crazy about you too."

"I was happy to see that you and Jack had so much in common," I said.

"He's an incredible guy. Speaking of which, dear," he paused, "I wanted to ask you something. Or, I should say, I wanted to ask your *permission* for something."

"I'm all ears."

"Well," he hesitated, "I'm a member of a few veterans' groups. I wanted to ask if it would be okay with you if I did a little checking. Nothing fancy, just a small military background check."

"Okay," I said slowly.

"Don't get me wrong," JC said. "Jack is a great guy…but I know you're an even greater girl, and I think the world of you. I just want to make sure everything's on the up and up, and you're with someone who is what he says he is."

"I guess I understand. Mom always said to trust

the cashier, but count your change."

"Exactly!" he said. "I'm gonna need some information from you to get started." I didn't have Jack's social security number, but I provided his full name and everything I remembered from his driver license. "Ok. I'm gonna call my buddy. I should know something in about 2-3 weeks."

As the wheels of his research turned, I turned my sights homeward for a more important meeting. A Columbus Chinese restaurant served as the setting for my parents' first sighting of their future son-in-law. I was filled with anticipation, as was Jack, who told me during our drive, "I hope they like me. I know how important they are to you." Truer words were never spoken, for he was preparing to meet the two most important role models in my life. Not only did my parents have a successful marriage of over thirty-five years, but their four-week courtship gave me confidence that they would relate to the emotions that were quickly growing between us. My excitement grew as I saw them emerge from their car..."Jack, this is my mom, Vivian"..."my dad, Gary."

It was a lively dinner as we munched egg rolls and discussed every topic under the sun, including psychic visions and Jack's self-description as an "adrenaline junkie." "I love your daughter," Jack repeatedly assured my parents in fervent overkill. Our collective talkativeness kept us in our seats until the restaurant closed. As we strolled to our cars, Dad and I busied ourselves in small talk as Jack assured my mother of his unwavering support of my professional goals. "I'll support her in whatever she does," he vowed.

"Good. Rest assured, I'm not the type of mom who interferes in Melissa's life. She rarely talks to me about her relationships, unless it's important. One thing you need to be aware of, though," she explained softly, "if she starts talking to me about major problems, it's over."

Jack assured her that he'd guard my happiness as we said our final goodbyes before embarking on our return to northern Ohio. Then came his nervous inquiries. Did my parents like him? Did he talk about his military background too much? How did he come across? "Sorry. I just want your folks to accept me, especially if I might be a part of the family someday."

"They'll accept you as long as *I* do. Just worry about me liking you. That's more than enough for now, right?" I playfully jabbed him. Just days before, the idea of marriage had reared its head in our discussion, a fact we chose not to discuss openly that night as my folks had enough to digest. I assured Jack the right time would arrive.

The coming days brought frequent dialogues about marriage plans. Our intentions arrived as a surprise to those who were unaware of our courtship, but others, including my parents- remained cautiously supportive. Since neither of us followed a Christian philosophy, we had no interest in a church wedding. Our mutual distaste for convention left us with an obvious, albeit vulgar, notion. We decided that Las Vegas, the veritable "Sin City" and site of marital wipe-outs of Joan Collins, Britney Spears, and Michael Jordan, would also host our nuptials.

Excitement mixed with sadness in my heart, for the geographical distance would prevent our loved ones from attending- a sadness that Jack didn't appear to share at first, as he had few family members whose presence *he* desired. For a mere fifty dollars, I ensured that our chapel would broadcast our ceremony on-line. Yet this didn't fill the hole I felt with the impending absence of my parents, who would be reduced to mere spectators "munching popcorn" around a computer screen- an analogy aptly made my mother, whose concern was growing.

Days later Jack and I sat on my sofa. I spilled my mixed emotions. I made the mistake of adding that my sadness was echoed by my mother, whom he subtly portrayed as the purveyor of a guilt trip. "Well, that's your mom. Powerful stuff. It made you feel guilty, didn't it?"

I denied his manipulative allegation, and proposed that we wait a few months to get married, at least until we had the opportunity to include our loved ones....my parents, his sisters, the kids. His brow furrowed and his face fell, "You don't want to get married?"

As I assured him it wasn't the case, I became hooked in a manipulative conversational cycle that eventually became a predictable hallmark of our conversations: misrepresentation ("It made you feel guilty, didn't it?"), failure to validate my feelings, topical diversion, and projection of motives. Wash, rinse, spin. Maytag didn't have nearly as much predictability.

Since I viewed our interaction as a misunderstanding, I sought to clarify, the quintessential attorney response. I explained that I wanted to ensure the inclusion of everyone who occupied a special place in our lives. "This is our biggest step," I said, "and I want to share it with my family. We have other options. I can call the chapel tomorrow about their policy on postponements."

Seeing my firm resolve, he proposed a solution that won me over. "You know," he said thoughtfully, "You're right. I just don't think about that much because my family is dysfunctional. But you have a good relationship with your folks. Let's fly them out there, no matter what it takes. I'll do it myself. When we book our flights next week, I'll book theirs. I'll put it all on my credit card. What d'ya say?" With a one-two punch, this bold challenge knocked out my hesitation, enhanced his image as a generous mate, and ensured that our nuptials proceeded as scheduled.

I accepted his generosity without questioning why this largesse wasn't shared with his own children, but I needn't have explored far to find the answer. Including his kids would require giving them advance notice of our ceremony. In light of Linda's ongoing presence at his house, Jack couldn't afford for their youthful exuberance to spill unwanted beans to his steady girlfriend.

Amidst the chaos of flight plans and reservations, I found time to visit JC for the results of his research. "Well," he hesitated, "My friend ran Jack's information. He couldn't find anything."

"Couldn't find anything?" I asked.

"Right. No good news, no bad news. There's no information in our databases on him."

I scratched my head. "I'm not sure I understand."

"I don't know what to tell you, dear. It could mean that he served the government admirably, but not in the military. Maybe private contracting. It could mean that the computers lost information. Just couldn't find a darned thing."

Whether it was denial, love, or a mixture of both is a question I never fully answered, but one thing is sure. Despite nodding my head in response to his results, I never *heard* the ramifications of my friend's words. Never before had my selective hearing blocked information so painfully obvious. My denial edited his speech to neutrality: nothing good or bad, just a guy who must have served "admirably." This was the last red flag raised prior to our ceremony, but it would not be the last.

4. WHO'S YOUR DADDY?

I can see the destiny you sold
Turned into a shining band of gold.
- The Police, "Wrapped Around Your Finger"

I was never one a little girl who dreamed of an elaborate church wedding. At thirty-four, I was simply happy to marry the man I loved. The unconventionality of Las Vegas added excitement to our nuptials as our plans took shape and I shopped for a dress. I found my gold mine in an upscale suburban thrift shop: an ivory tea-length gown that flattered my frame and cost a mere thirty-four dollars.

It was far easier for me to dress myself for the event than it was for Jack to dress up our engagement in a cloak of deception. Back in Massillon he was forced, in the words of my profession, to "lay the foundation" for dropping the bombshell of our wedding to family and friends. His relationship with Linda required a level of secrecy unparalleled by the FBI, an organization for which he laid claim to several high-level contacts. Despite the fact he introduced me to his children, my contact with the youngsters was minimal compared to that of Linda, who was good friends with several other members of his family. Jack's gnawing fear grew. He'd *still* have to explain the existence of a new wife to his family. More importantly, he'd have to explain the existence of a new stepmother to his kids. Even worse, he'd need to explain why those two roles were not going to be fulfilled by Linda, but by me. His predicament required him to craft an identity for me that justified a sudden marriage.

He'd already begun to craft this identity with Linda, a captive audience for his lurid tale of being pursued by an obsessed "other" woman. He slowly added features to this neurotic siren that lent credence to his tale of victimization: obsessive, younger than he, moderately attractive, and far more desirous of a serious relationship than Jack himself. Her education level was sketchy, a probable high school graduate who happened to work in a profession for which he held a deep fascination: exotic dancing. And so it came to pass that this hapless stripper, addled by her fatal attraction for Jack, attributed her pregnancy to him. He decided to convince this manipulative strumpet to undergo an abortion, which provided a viable excuse to Linda for his continued contact with her in the weeks that preceded his Vegas excursion. If he met her "to talk," then he could keep her satisfied enough that she'd agree to the procedure.

By the time Jack crafted this alternate identity for me, I'd morphed from an articulate attorney into a mentally unstable stripper who used her pregnancy to pressure him into a committed relationship. The laughable fiction was a grandiose exercise that diverted his **own** manipulative tendencies onto a woman and later provided a justification for his nuptials.

Just as he crafted my alter ego for Linda's benefit, Jack also had to create a misinformation campaign for me. I was told that he couldn't tell his kids about our ceremony, because they'd tell their mother Theresa. He couldn't tell Theresa herself, for her vindictiveness carried ramifications for his relationship with their kids, not to mention any monkey wrenches she might throw into our trip, e.g, refusing to keep the kids during his absence. He couldn't tell Linda, because her jealousy would blow the roof off their "friendship." The only individuals in whom he was free to confide were his dog Minnie, his cat Sammie, and co-workers at the radio station, where he served as a supplier of "non-traditional revenue."

Although I generally believed his misinformation campaign, I questioned the rationale for the secrecy with Linda. It seemed extreme, a fact I pointed out to him. "For an independent woman who dates guys regularly, she seems unnaturally attached to you. You guys never dated at all or had sex, right? I'd understand if your hormones got out of control once. Sometimes women attach significance to sex that guys don't, and it's hard to revert to platonic friendship afterward."

"No, no, no," he maintained. "It wasn't like that. We didn't have sex. I give you my word. She's just a well-meaning woman, but very insecure. What matters more to me right now is us."

Along with secretive wedding plans, I was forced to address the failing health of a beloved pet, my eldest cat Burbles. Her plummeting weight and digestive upsets concerned me, for the steroids that sustained her during the previous year were losing their effectiveness. Nevertheless, I ensured that Burbles had the best care in my absence, voluntarily provided by my colleague and fellow cat owner Pam. I carefully lined up Burbles' medication and supplies, with instructions for Pam, along with the phone number of Burbles' vet. Not even the excitement of our ceremony quelled the concern I felt as I looked into her cloudy eyes and petted her frail body. "It'll be ok, Burbs. Mommy's coming back soon," I assured her.

If ignorance is truly bliss, then I was in virtual nirvana when we boarded our flight at Akron-Canton Airport that warm May day. Landing in Las Vegas, I was agog at the sights and sounds of a city built on conspicuous consumption and risk-taking. I was about to take a risk far higher than the high rollers sipping on Tangueray at the blackjack tables. In less than forty-eight hours, my high-stakes bet would be placed at the Little White Wedding Chapel.

Jack and I slept in the following morning at the Days Inn. After indulging in one of the city's many breakfast buffets, we proceeded to the Clark County Marriage Bureau, where we took our place in line with a diverse crowd awaiting the chance to purchase their marital lottery ticket. Couples in their fifties joined twenty-somethings in this veritable melting pot of lovers.

Once we arrived at the clerk's window, we were placed on the assembly line. "Groom?" she asked, looking at Jack, whose nod prompted rapid fire questioning.

"Full name," she demanded succinctly. Jack Alan Cass.

"City of residence." Massillon, Ohio.

"Date of birth." August 23, 1961.

"State of birth." Ohio.

"Marital status." Divorced.

"When." October 29, 1999.

"Where." Canton, Ohio.

"Number of this marriage." Two.

On she went until my turn arrived. I spit out the information as quickly as her fingers typed.

As we exited the marriage bureau, I took several glances at our permission slip. "Affidavit of Application for Marriage License, No. D687202." It sounded official. As I skipped down the concrete steps, I was unaware that the document contained proof that Jack was beginning our marriage with two key lies: his age and number of marriages. Although our affidavit reflected that I was marrying a 42-year-old man with one prior marriage (to Theresa), I was *actually* marrying a 45-year-old man who'd been divorced twice: once from Dina, and again from Theresa. The fact that I was bride number three isn't a fact that would have repelled me from Jack, had he been honest. His duplicity, however, rendered the document tangible evidence of fraud. As we returned to the hotel to await my parents' arrival, I was unaware that I held a legal basis for a future annulment.

When our phone rang, I smiled. I breathed easier with the knowledge that my parents were in town to join me for the occasion. With Jack in tow, I raced to their room and hugged them hello. I plopped down on their bed as we discussed their flight and turned our attention to the evening's dinner plans.

We exchanged stories around a hibachi table at Caesar's famous Hyakumi restaurant as we watched their artisan grill and toss food with exquisite grace. As nearby diners retired to the casino, Jack referenced both his family and military history, describing the experiences he claimed molded his personality and instill him with sound values. My parents related to his turbulent relationship with his father, and we listened with empathy to Jack's mythic portraits in courage.

Our conversation continued at the hotel, where we gathered in my parents' room for a few final words. "Well," Mom eventually said, "you've got a big day tomorrow. We want to be awake to enjoy it. All of us should probably get some sleep."

After we awoke to another breakfast buffet, Jack retired to my parents' room as Mom came to ours to help me prepare for the ceremony. Thirty years after I sat on her bed choking on hairspray, Mom stepped gingerly out of the bathroom doorway as my own chemical mist spewed into the atmosphere. Placement of my veil became our most challenging exercise in this ritual, as each of us struggled to insert the veil's comb into my hair. After finding a suitable position, we checked my accessories. Something old (my mother's class ring), something new (my veil and ivory scarf wrap), something borrowed (pearl choker from my colleague), and something blue (my garter). I was good to go. We called the room where Jack and Dad busied themselves.

We heard a knock. In walked Dad and Jack, whose eyes didn't stray once they set upon me. "Wow," he exhaled, as his hand raised to his chest and slid down his lapel in an absentminded grooming gesture. "I'm not worthy," he said.

"Probably not," my mom observed with a wry smile. "But *she* seems to think so."

The phone rang. At the end of the line was the driver of our chapel's limousine. "Good afternoon," she said. "We're outside your hotel."

As we rolled up in front of the Little White Chapel, our eyes were greeted with couples clad in a variety of wedding attire. Conventional bridal gowns and tuxedos peppered the sea of denim jeans and leather that lined the chapel's sidewalks. Once inside the lobby, we approached the counter, where a kind woman took our names and asked us to wait patiently until staff ensured that the webcam and video recorder were set up. A tan bald gentleman clad in a suit came into the lobby and introduced himself.

"Good afternoon. I'm Reverend Ron Porras, and I'll be performing your ceremony this afternoon," he said in a thick Hispanic accent. He shook our hands with each of us. "You are the groom, I presume? Bride? And you are the bride's parents. Nice to meet you." He directed us into the small chapel, where he introduced Jack and me to the organist, a courteous woman in her early sixties who inquired about our spiritual background.

"Do you prefer Christian music, or just general?" she asked pleasantly.

"Just general," we replied in unison.

"No problem," she said, as my parents were directed to sit on a bench in the chapel's front.

Shortly I heard the bridal march begin. As I walked down the aisle, each step seemed like forever as I became amazed at how my thirty-four years had culminated in this moment.

"We are gathered here today to join Jack and Melissa in holy matrimony."

For his own part, Jack remained steady while I tearfully stumbled through promising to "comfort" him. It was virtually impossible for me to gauge the reactions of computer users across northeast Ohio when Rev. Porras beckoned objectors to "speak now or forever hold your peace." Although he was too much of a gentleman to reveal it, I'm positive that JB and the crew voiced a few wry observations at that juncture.

Following the pronouncement of Jack and me as "husband and wife," Rev. Porras gave us an opportunity to say a few words to those watching on-line. I saluted my loved ones and colleagues, while Jack gave a shout to his kids and "the folks at Rock 107."

Suddenly, an awkward pause fell over the chapel as we giggled and Jack said, "Well, uh, there is one more thing I wanted to say." Our growing laughter made it hard to conceal our inside joke. Without further adieu, Jack turned my backside towards the camera, gently swatted my derriere, and said, "Who's your daddy?!?" Mom's jaw dropped.

It was the one-liner heard 'round the internet, or at least 'round computer terminals in northeast Ohio. While it was a source of consternation for some of my family members, It became a continual punch line at juvenile court, where probation officers, fellow magistrates, and detention employees alike greeted me with, "G'morning, Magistrate Dean. Who's your daddy?" In the meantime, it raised the eyebrows of Rev. Porras, whose stunned reaction to our comedic stunt seemed uncharacteristic of a minister whose repertoire included drive-thru weddings and nuptials serenaded by Elvis impersonators.

After we received our official marriage certificate,

we proceeded to the chapel's photography studio. Eventually I had several favorites enlarged for us and other family members. Interestingly, none of these enlargements ever earned a space among Jack's family photos on the walls at his homestead on Navarre Road. My future attempts to hang our wedding pictures were met with concern that I would not accomplish the task correctly. "Don't do it until I'm there," he often declared. That time never arrived- at least, not until after my first separation from Jack.

Although we hadn't determined where to dine, Mom and Dad graciously offered to treat us to our wedding night meal. We directed the cabbie to take us to the Venetian, which offered a variety of fine dining options. Jack and I settled on Delmonico Steakhouse, owned and operated by none other than celebrity chef Emeril Lagasse.

Shortly after we began feasting on our entrees, Jack laid his fork down and looked up suddenly. "I just realized something," he said thoughtfully.

"What's that?" I asked.

"It's Theresa's birthday today," he said. "Her birthday's May 29, and here we are."

"Bam!" I thought in Emeril-like fashion. Instead, I heard, "Really?" emerge from my lips. "I hope she's having a decent time with the kids."

Just *why* Jack felt it appropriate to inject this family trivia into our wedding night dinner escaped me. It was an ironic observation coming from a man who frequently responded to questions with a sheepish, "Ah I'm not good with dates." I looked on the bright side of his etiquette breach: At least I stood a good chance that he'd always remember my birthday!

After dinner, we returned to my parents' hotel room, where we held a brief Jack-centric conversation. Their yawns grew more frequent, and their return trip loomed the following day. Jack and I retired to our room.

Given the excitement of our trip, it was easy to forget that our return to Ohio coincided with Memorial Day, the reminders of which decorated televisions at the airport. It was an ever-present reality for my new husband, whose alleged military service endowed him with a resonance for veterans who paid the ultimate sacrifice. Our return flight was littered with military references and somber recollections of a comrade dying in his arms. Such memories, he claimed, were often jogged by special occasions like Memorial Day.

"Guys like me, we never got parades and honors," he motioned toward the television screen. "Fellows in special ops can't receive public recognition. We have to stay anonymous. We're the expendable ones. It's alright, though, 'cause we didn't serve to get glory." Even my brief bout with airsickness was met with his playful gibe, "Remind me never to take you on a C-130!"

We landed at the Akron-Canton Airport shortly after daybreak. As we rolled in to the driveway that was now *ours*, we planned our schedule for the coming few days. Despite our new marital status, my physical move to Massillon was still in transition, with over half of my belongings still at my Elyria apartment. As Jack placed my luggage in my car, I told him that I'd call him later that evening after checking on Burbles.

"I should probably get this lawn mowed," he said, scanning the property. "If I start in the next hour, I might get it done by about seven or so."

We agreed that I'd bring more belongings later in the week. Large furniture items would wait until Jack secured his father's truck. In the meantime, we kissed goodbye in what seemed like an anticlimactic end to a momentous occasion. Jack waved goodbye in my rearview mirror.

When I walked in my door, I called out to my feline friends. Young gray Artemis bounced into the living room, but Burbles was nowhere to be seen. Then her black and white face slowly appeared from behind the sofa. Her thin frame walked gingerly towards me, struggling for each step. To save her effort, I approached my ailing cat and petted her, my face wincing in anguish at her protruding spine. "How are you baby?" I asked, as she managed a faint purr.

As I walked into the kitchen, I saw a note from Pam. She described my cat's continual difficulty keeping food down. "I never recall seeing her this thin!" she wrote. I sank into the kitchen chair as the magnitude of Burbles' condition hit me. It wasn't the first time I'd seen a cat of mine struck down with terminal illness without warning. At that point, I didn't need a diagnostic test to tell me what was necessary. I picked up my cordless phone and dialed my vet's number.

"Amherst Animal Hospital, can I help you?"

"My cat Burbles was just there about a month ago," I said. "She's bad off, and she's lost a lot of weight. She's vomiting dark stuff. She can barely walk...." I stammered.

"Would you like to bring her in for an exam? The doctor can reevaluate her medication."

I cleared my throat. "I don't know how to say this, but she's beyond medication. She's alive, but she's not living. I can't see her like this anymore."

The receptionist's voice grew softer, "I'm so sorry. Would you prefer to make an appointment to have her euthanized?"

"Yes," I replied.

"When would you like to bring her in?"

"As soon as possible," I said firmly.

"I can get her in at nine tomorrow morning. Is that alright?"

"Sure," as I thanked the universe I was off work the following day.

As Burbles lay quietly, I called Jack to let him know, but couldn't get an answer at the house or on his cell. Those without a deep bond to pets couldn't relate to my mood; however, I needed the ear of the one I loved. As a companion to two animals himself, I was sure Jack could empathize with my impending loss. I cursed the lawn care for taking my new husband's attention, but I was cursing the wrong thing.

It wasn't growing grass, but rather his growing deception, that hampered Jack's availability that day. Following his return from Las Vegas, he had serious business to take care of. Scarcely two hours after we kissed goodbye in the driveway, Jack went to Linda's house. Like most Americans, she was off work Memorial Day, and undoubtedly eager to see whether her boyfriend's out-of-state excursion with his pregnant strumpet yielded fruit. Did he convince her to have the abortion? After he reassured her of his success, the two talked and did what comes naturally to two lovers in a steady relationship. Barely forty-eight hours after pledging fidelity to me at the Little White Wedding Chapel, Jack and Linda had sex. Instead of breaking the news of our marriage to her, the pseudo-SEAL and paragon of bravery waited for someone else to drop his brutal bomb.

Jack eventually called that night, offering his condolences.

"I wish you could go with me tomorrow," I said.

"I'm sorry. I gotta go back to work tomorrow." After a brief monologue about animal life, he offered his condolences again and wished me goodnight. "I love you," he said.

"I love you, too."

I carried Burbles to my bed. This was her last

night, and I didn't want her immobility to prevent her from being near me. Despite her difficulties, she got down once to use the litter box, but laid down in the hallway instead of returning to the bed. After stumbling to the restroom, I checked her in the moonlight to verify that her chest was rising and falling. I stroked her head and laid back down for three more sleepless hours.

My alarm sounded. I wasted no time. I gently wrapped Burbles' scrawny frame in a towel and carried her out the door.

"Oh dear," said the veterinary attendant. "She feels like a bag of bones. I'm going to take her in the back and let Dr. Mark prep her."

Moments later, they returned to the exam room. I didn't let the vet tell me how much she weighed. "That's understandable. I can tell you she's lost weight in the month since she was here. I could perform more tests to locate the underlying problem, but that could traumatize her further. She's clearly dealing with a terminal condition," he said. He explained the mechanics of her "final shot." He asked if I preferred to remain in the room for the procedure; I said yes.

As the vet positioned his needle on her leg, I knelt beside the exam table, lowering my face in front of hers. It was my firm belief that her last vision shouldn't be a stranger in a white coat, but rather her human companion. As her eyes closed, I gave her a brief kiss as my salty tear fell onto her fur. The vet placed his stethoscope over her chest and nodded. "Okay," he whispered.

I was slapped with the stifling humidity as I walked into the parking lot. At home, I lit a candle for my furry friend's memory, then set about to the awesome task of packing my belongings.

It was a breezy June afternoon when Linda received an unwanted phone call at her desk. It was one of Jack's aunts. "Is everything okay with you and Jack?" she asked.

"Yeah, why?"

Linda could hardly believe her ears as Jack's aunt directed her to go on-line and check the webcam archives for the Little White Wedding Chapel. She watched her boyfriend promise to love, honor and cherish another woman, only to salute his kids and co-workers at the ceremony's end. In the space of five minutes, Jack made a mockery of the love, energy, and financial resources she provided him for over two years.

Still reeling, Linda was savvy enough to realize she had to act fast to protect herself from further loss. Her rose-colored glasses ripped off with violent force, she was painfully aware that she couldn't count on Jack to keep his word to pay his financial debt as promised. Meanwhile, her debts mounted and her mortgage beckoned. After waiting a few days to cool off, she sat down and wrote a promissory note documenting Jack's debt and asked him to meet her for lunch. With his new wife still living in Elyria, he was free to meet Linda for lunch without scrutiny.

Jack strode confidently into the restaurant and sat down. Despite her nervous tension, Linda tried to maintain his comfort level with small talk before turning it to the subject of money.

He remain unfazed when she pulled out the promissory note, and signed it without incident. Three weeks into his marriage, Jack had no qualm signing a financial document without his attorney wife's knowledge. But he did have a problem telling the truth.

His brow furrowed quizzically as he noticed Linda scanning his arms and hands. "What are you looking at?"

"Just looking," she shrugged, "....for your wedding band."

"What?! What are you talking about? I'm not

married." He maintained that his mini-vacation was designed to convince his manipulative companion into an abortion.

"Look," he said. "I had to take her away somewhere so that I could get some sense in her. I didn't want you to be hurt. Doesn't mean that I married her!"

"Oh, really?" Linda asked.

"You bet," Jack snapped with growing agitation.

Linda leaned forward. *"Who's your daddy?!"*

Jack's face turned ashen. Linda stood to leave.

"Linda, wait. You don't understand. I had to. It's not valid anyway. I didn't give them the right info for the license."

"Just shut up." Undaunted, she walked out.

5. TOSS IT ALL

They crawled out of the woodwork
And they whispered into your brain.
They set you on the treadmill
And they made you change your name.
- Elton John, "Candle in the Wind"

The welcome mat of deception paved the way for my transition as I moved my belongings to the Massillon residence that was now my marital home. The summer heat didn't make our efforts easier as Jack and I lugged boxes into the house dubbed by neighbors as "the place with the pond." As we sweated through our rigors, Jack bemoaned his lack of air conditioning.

"The central air broke down a couple years ago. Never had the money to get it fixed."

Moving into the bedroom posed a unique challenge. The existence of two closets made it easy to delineate our space, but the hard part was the cleaning. The closet we designated as mine contained shoes, clothing, and mementos belonging to Jack's second wife Theresa.

"Sorry. I shoulda cleaned this out for you long before you moved in," he said with a blasé sigh. "When she left several years ago, she left more crap than I realized."

"That was 1999. You mean to tell me you haven't touched this closet in four years?" I said incredulously, my newlywed diplomacy cracking under the strain of amazement. Squinting at the disheveled space, I pulled out a white cotton "NY & Co." baseball cap with the tag still attached. I carefully plucked chards of broken glass from the floor. Seconds later, I found the culprit: an old wedding photo of Jack and Theresa with a cracked frame. I raised it for Jack's viewing pleasure.

"Any ideas on what to do with this?" I asked, my left eyebrow cocked upward.

"Oh my. Honey, I'm sorry! It's garbage as far as I'm concerned," he said, holding the black Hefty bag open for me. Pausing in the bedroom doorway, he said, "You know, that's *your* space. Do whatever you want with it. Throw everything out if you wish. Just toss it all."

"The problem," I sighed, "is that I can't tell if some of these things are family mementos. Maybe the kids should have some of this. I don't know what's here. Heck, I don't know if Jimmy Hoffa's in here." I moved a pile of debris aside, only to be startled by the crackle of flimsy plastic. "That's the kind of assessment *you* need to make, Jack." I pulled out a clear plastic display box containing a wedding cake server, complete with a white ribbon bow.

"I don't need anything from that era. I trust your judgment. Just toss it all," he maintained.

"Okay, but I just don't wanna hear anything later, like 'Where's Mommy's old whatchamacallit?'"I said, extricating a pair of new white pumps from the rubbish.

"Her wedding shoes. Guess they didn't mean much to her," he shrugged. "Toss it all, hon. I'm gonna run downstairs and make us some dinner."

Toss it all. That was the only input given by my husband, whose proffering of dinner allowed him to evade the closet cleaning in an ostensibly even exchange of chores. Yet the ramifications were anything but even, as I sorted thru memories that didn't belong to me. It seemed a trivializing gesture towards a stage of his life that merited a modicum of respect. Somewhere in the region of my subconscious lay the notion that if "for better or worse" led to the worse part, Jack would eventually have some other woman toss *my* personal effects.

As I ventured into the bathroom to store my health and beauty aids, I encountered the same input from Jack: Toss it all. Bottles of hair spray, cosmetics, and miscellaneous accessories lined the cabinet interior. I wiped away globs of dark goo that leaked from unidentifiable tubes of cosmetics. On the top shelf I found a hand-held cosmetic purse caddy, an item Jack later attributed to Linda rather than Theresa. The array of items belonging to these women were tossed in the black Hefty bag I retrieved from our kitchen.

For reasons I never understood, not once did I consider pressing Jack to assume responsibility for this "out with the old, in with the new" cleaning ritual. From that point on, I tacitly agreed to clean up his messes in the name of marital unity, literally *and* metaphorically. Once I cleared the bathroom shelves, I situated my belongings, carefully arranging the array of washcloths and towels given to me by my parents. Aside from the basement where I exercised, the small cubicle where I showered eventually became one of my refuges from domestic dysfunction. Those towels were the solitary balm that dried my body after continual showers of negativity and anger. Just as the water washed the venom away, those simple pieces of cloth enveloped me in a cocoon of loving care. I had no idea of the significance they would assume.

The array of cosmetics and clothes in my inventory captured the range of roles I played. The suits and muted eye shadow worn by the attorney and Bhutto-esque intellectual contrasted with the daring tops and form-fitting ensembles worn by the wife on a date with her husband. And there were the bikinis, leather and dramatic make-up, all hallmarks of the V-Twin Girl "Kitten" he later created, reminiscent of Anna Nicole. Despite the admiration he initially expressed for my wide range, his appreciation dissipated and the selections that I used slowly narrowed to suit Jack's fancy. This wasn't accomplished with the same terse instruction with which he dispatched Theresa's belongings. Had he thrown all my sporty and conservative selections onto the floor with disdain, "Toss it all" would've evoked an immediate response from me. Rather, it was a slow process, one that began with compliments and flattery.

"You know," he said several weeks after our wedding, "You're so beautiful. I'd love to take some pictures of you outside. It's a lovely day. You wanna?"

"Sure, but...why?"

"You're my wife," he said. "I love how you look, especially in those Daisy Dukes. Plus I love the outdoors. I wanna get some shots of the property out front, too."

"Ok," I said, as I donned my American flag halter top and Daisy Dukes. After striking a few poses near a tree in our back yard, I wondered around the property as he took photos of the pond.

"You, know," I mused, "this is such a beautiful pond. We should come out here one fall morning, sit on the bench and have coffee together."

"Sounds good. I love doing this!" he gushed. "I used to take nature photos when I did outdoor features for the local paper. I'm a pro."

"That's cool, hon," I said, slapping bugs away from my legs. "I'm gonna head in. I'm getting eaten alive out here."

"Wait," he said. "I'm almost done. Don't you want to be out here with me?"

I sighed, and stared as my beloved shutterbug completed his duties. I was caught off-guard by Jack's subtle yet distinctive emotional blackmail. With few words, he transformed my reluctance to become bug food into something about *him* and evaded my discomfort. It wasn't the first time, for just a few months ago he had responded similarly to my desire to include family in our wedding: "You don't want to get married?" Already there was a pattern, and I was following it.

The pattern continued as Jack and I settled into the daily rituals of wedded bliss. Each day I arose at 5:15 am, brushed my teeth, and hurried out the door by 6:30 to drive an hour and fifteen minutes to Elyria. On most mornings I made coffee prior to my departure, a gesture Jack reciprocated on the weekends. After eight hours of conducting child support hearings and juvenile justice cases, I returned to Massillon by 5:30. Since Jack worked closer to home, he usually prepared dinner, after which I retired to the basement to exercise at least forty-five minutes. After my shower, I often looked forward to flopping on the sofa for a daily dose of mindless drivel from the boob tube. By 10:30 I was ready to drop.

One June evening, Jeff emerged from the computer room and paused in the doorway to our den. "Guess what?" he asked. "Theresa's starting a rumor that you're pregnant."

"Really?" I asked.

"Yeah! She watched the wedding video on her computer. She thinks you looked pregnant or something. When I talked with her today on the phone, she said, 'So when's she due?'" When I mused about her inaccuracy, Jack passed it off as his ex-wife's negative spirit. "I don't know how she could say something like that. But that's the way she is. She's catty and vengeful."

It was now his jealous ex Theresa who was the rumor-starter in this elaborate tale, rather than Jack himself. This brilliant transfer allowed him to inoculate me from the truth by giving me a heads up that his tawdry lie was floating around Stark County.

"Ah well," I said from my sofa perch. "Not much I can do about that. By the way. We need to take a look at our bills. I get paid this week, so I can start sharing a few expenses."

"Good," he sighed with relief. "We're gonna

need it!"

"Why do you say it like that? Is everything okay?"

"Yeah," he said. "It's just that the mortgage is due this week, and I don't think my paycheck from the radio station will cover it."

"You don't *think* it will, or you *know* it won't?" I asked.

"Well, the house payment is eleven hundred, and after child support & taxes, my check is less than that."

"Okay," I said, "that's good to know. What date of the month is the mortgage due?"

"By the tenth," he said.

"Does that mean the payment itself is due on the tenth, or do you pay it by that date to avoid extra charges? There's a difference between the due date and the end of a grace period." My bankruptcy had taught me brutal lessons.

"After the tenth, the payment goes way up. Can't remember how much it jumps, though."

I sighed as I flipped through channels. The members of congress blathering endlessly on C-SPAN had more budgetary awareness than my new husband. Maybe I was just more attuned to detail than he. Although I tried to overlook this as a mere difference in our personalities, I couldn't avoid furrowing my brow in confusion. My facial movement didn't go unnoticed.

"What? Did I say something wrong?" he asked.

"No," I replied. "I guess I'm just confused." I sat up on the sofa pillow, my head cocked. "You helped build this house with a veteran's loan during your days with Dina. You've lived here for twenty years. It surprises me that you don't know specific terms of your mortgage."

"Theresa took care of that!" Jack said indignantly. "Plus, these 'terms' changed over the years. When she screwed me in the divorce, I had to take out another loan to pay her half of the house. The payments went up. Everything went up except my income! Everything always changes except me. Women change their mind. Companies change rates. I stay the same."

"Okay," I sighed. "I'll deposit my check this Friday and we'll look at the mortgage later." Since the finance company didn't use monthly coupon books, it was hard to discern Jack's payment history. Upon examining the statement days later, I realized he was a month behind, just like the gas bill. Not only did I walk into a web of deception, but I moved into a financial morass as messy as his ex-wife's closet. I realized I'd made a tactical error by not exploring our financial status before we married. After all, "I'm not a rich man" is hardly a descriptive index of one's financial status, and I could've inquired further. We were behind to the tune of one month's expenses when the ink was still drying on our marriage certificate.

While I was being slapped with my new financial status, my new stepchildren were being slapped with the news they had a stepmother, and it wasn't Linda. Several times, young Jill raised uncomfortable questions for Jack as we watched television.

"Daddy, why doesn't Linda come over anymore?"

"Because I don't need Linda anymore. I have Melissa," was his typical response.

It's impossible for me to gauge the thoughts of young minds forced into a blended family unit so suddenly. During courtship, Jack and I discussed our blended family in vague terms of "teamwork." I told him that I considered my role as stepmother akin to that of a vice-president, while he and Theresa served as the presidents, i.e., the main authority figures. I loved and cared for them, without a desire to usurp authority from their biological parents. Like the vice-president, my authority would only be summoned on an as-needed basis. At least, that's how I saw it. Jack agreed.

Although they were over at our house only three nights each week, I tried to bond with Jill and Jason within their own comfort zone. I watched television with the kids and helped Jill with her homework and reading assignments. "It's okay. When we stumble on big words, we just take it slower."

It was a contrast to Jack's approach, whose impatience drove him to spit out words in her materials or urge her along. Interestingly, he didn't read as impatiently when the subject matter captured his attention. One July day, he brought home a monthly entertainment newspaper that featured local clubs, bands, and various recreational events throughout Stark County.

"Check this out," he said. "I picked it up at the station. It's an entertainment paper. It lists a lot of local events. There's an ad in here that's pretty interesting. I wanted to show it to you."

"What is it?" I asked as I walked over to the dining room table.

"Just look," he said with the excitement of a little boy. "Look in the upper right hand corner. There's an ad for a photographer in Dover. I think may be able to do some things for us."

"What are you talking about?" I inquired quizzically.

Looking at the paper, I saw an ad for Tumbleweed Photography Studio featuring the work of Noel Croswell, whose repertoire included weddings, family settings, glamour shots, and boudoir photos. Most importantly for Jack, the ad featured a photo of an attractive young woman clad in jeans astride a motorcycle. "Specializing in bikes and babes," it read.

"It's a nice ad," I said. "Sounds like the photographer has a wide range. But what do we need him to do *for* us?"

"Look," Jack said, "I'm sure you're prettier than any girl he's ever worked with. You'd look great on those bikes. Remember how you told me you've always been curious about modeling? This could be a good way to get your feet wet." When I mentioned that I wasn't young or tall enough to hit the runways, he protested, "Not every model struts down a runway. Biker models are becoming popular, because motorcycles are growing in popularity. It's not like this would be a full-time job or anything. If this guy puts you in a few shoots, it could lead to something bigger if you want it to. If not, you don't have to do it anymore. Why don't I give him a call?"

"Eh, I don't know," I hesitated. In all my years, I'd never considered to apply the term "model" to myself.

"I'm telling' ya, this guy works with the motorcycle community, and that's a hot concept right now. You on a bike would be a vision."

"I don't know about *that*," I explained.

"Well, I do," he declared. "How 'bout I give this Noel guy a call, just to see what he's about? I won't even call about modeling. I'll call like it's radio business, to see if he's interested in advertising. That way I can find out more."

I arrived home from work the following Friday to hear Jack explain that he had a meeting scheduled with Noel Croswell the following day. "Noel wants to meet us for lunch tomorrow."

"Why *us*?" I asked. "I thought you were gonna hit him up like an radio ad rep first, do a little investigation."

"I talked with him," he insisted. "He sounds legit. He wants to meet us tomorrow at the Hog Heaven in New Philadelphia."

"Sounds like you already explored the modeling idea with him," I observed. "Thought you might've talked with me first about what you learned in your 'investigation.'"

"It's not a high-end networking meeting," he said as he talked *past* my admonition. "Don't worry. Again…it's not something you have to commit to." Yet the liberties Jack had already taken signaled the fertilization of an idea that took root in his brain days before our conversation.

As we walked into restaurant, we saw a silver-haired bearded gentleman sitting at the bar with an attractive young brunette with dramatic eye makeup. "I think that's him," Jack whispered.

At that moment, the gentleman turned around and everyone introduced themselves.

"Hi, I'm Noel," he said jovially as each of us shook his hand. "This is Maria; she's one of my models."

"Hi," said the woman as she shook our hand.

After several minutes of small talk, Noel explained his goals for the photography studio, and his desire to gain more exposure in the motorcycle community. "From Easyrider Magazine to local bike runs, it's a big market. The two most favorite things to those guys are bikes and girls. Everyone wants to see a pretty woman on a motorcycle."

"I couldn't agree more," Jack said, nodding in agreement. "That's an interest for us, too. I love to ride… course, I don't have my bike anymore. But I agree. The whole "bikes and babes" thing is hot. Over at the radio station, I've been trying to introduce a 'bikes and babes' style page on their site. You know, kinda like other Ohio radio stations do a 'Girl of the Month' or something similar. The station manager is a conservative woman in her fifties, and she ain't buying it."

"I can imagine," Noel said.

"I finally decided I'm going to take the idea elsewhere, branch out on my own, maybe a separate website altogether. Melissa is interested in doing a bit of modeling," Jack said, motioning in my direction. "I saw your ad and figured we should talk. I think we can work together."

"Definitely, definitely," Noel nodded.

The two men tossed around promotional ideas like a volleyball. Noel rolled out a poster of Maria seated atop a Harley-Davidson.

"That's a perfect concept," Jack said. "Would you be interested in doing a shoot in the near future? Melissa could come out. Maybe she and Maria could team up in a few pictures." Maria nodded excitedly as I pondered the idea. It sounded intriguing, even kind of fun.

"I don't know about your studio schedule, but we're free on the weekends," Jack said.

"I get a lot of weddings this time of year," Noel replied. "Next month is better. How 'bout the second Saturday in August?"

Jack turned to me. "Is that okay with you?"

"Sure, why not?" I replied.

As we drove home, Jack asked, "Well, how do ya feel? You looking forward to it?"

"Sorta," I said. "You could say I'm looking forward, but a bit nervous at the same time."

"Why? You're in great shape. Couldn't hurt to put in some extra treadmill time the next few days, just to be your best. But I don't think you need much work at all. You look great!"

A couple weeks later, I awoke Saturday morning to a pleasant rural breeze and the aroma of hazelnut coffee. As I sat up in bed, Jack walked in the bedroom with a coffee cup in hand.

"Here's my baby's morning coffee," he said as he put the mug down beside me.

"Thanks, hon," I said, as I retrieved my java from the ledge of Jack's gun cabinet. The structure served as my makeshift night stand, holding everything from coffee to hair pins. It never occurred to me to ponder the negative ramifications of this placement. Feng shui practitioners would surely flee in horror from a room where firearms graced the space designated for peaceful slumber and marital intimacy. The energy introduced by these instruments was unmistakable to any outside observer, but it remained unrecognizable to me.

"Mmm," I said groggily, gazing at the rifles and handguns. "This is good coffee."

"Yeah, that Eight O'clock brand ain't bad. Oh, by the way... Theresa's coming over in a few to pick up the kids. We'll have plenty of time for you to get ready before we leave. You comin' downstairs or takin' a shower first?"

"I'm coming downstairs to get some water, maybe grab some breakfast. Then I'll shower."

"Alright. I wouldn't eat anything too heavy," he warned. "You don't wanna feel bloated right before the shoot."

Bloat? It never occurred to me. I wasn't in the habit of eating heavy breakfasts anyway. Although he framed it in a manner reflecting concern for how I *feel*, it later became easy for me to grasp that Jack's real concern was how I *looked*. From that moment on, the fear of "bloat" never left my brain when I prepared for the camera.

We arrived at Noel's studio to find a set carefully arranged with a Harley in place. The aroma of stale smoke hit me as I peered at the glamour shots lining his office.

"Where's Maria?" I asked, looking around for my partner.

"She couldn't make it," Noel said. "Had to cancel at the last minute."

"That's too bad," I mused.

I retired to the dressing room. Opening my duffel bag, I paused. I called for Jack. "I can't decide which one to wear first," I said, motioning towards my bag. "Which one do you think?"   "The white bikini," he said fervently. "And those clear heels."

After donning my bikini, I checked my hair and refreshed my lipstick before slowly emerging into the studio. I shivered as I tried to rub my goose bumps away.

"Wow... you look great!" Jack and Noel said in unison

"I'm gonna do a few test shots beforehand, to get a feel for the lighting," Noel said.

"Okay, here we go," he said, as he suggested a few different poses. Noel made small talk as I twisted and turned. "So what kind of work do you normally do?" he asked me.

Jack and I exchanged all-knowing smirks. "I'm a lawyer," I said.

"You're kidding me!" he exclaimed, moving his camera to the right, then the left.

"No, but I play one on television," I quipped.

Noel dragged a fan behind his lights. "We're gonna try this for a different effect," he said, flipping the switch.

My curly hair flew backward like numerous models whose hair fluttered in the breeze of carefully situated fans. I liked the feeling of my hair being off my face. With Noel's patience and helpful suggestions, I grew more comfortable in front of the camera, occasionally suggesting new poses and facial positions. A few more wardrobe changes here, photo snaps, and I was finished.

"I'll call you Thursday when I get the proofs back," Noel said as Jack and I walked out.

"Well, how did ya feel?" Jack said on our way home.

"It was weird at first, but eventually I had more fun," I said. "Sitting on a Harley is a lot different than sitting at my desk," I said, "it was a nice little break."

The following weekend we returned to Noel's studio. "You guys are gonna love these," he said excitedly. "I don't think I've ever worked with someone as photogenic."

"Thank you," I said, blushing as Jack leafed through the snapshots.

"These are great! You look beautiful, hon."

"Uggh," I blurted at the sight of an unflattering angle.

"Don't worry. Only about ten to fifteen percent of shots like this ever get used. Can't get 'em all perfect. One of them turned out so good I'm gonna blow it up into a poster so we can take it to a few local places. I'll see if you spot the one I'm talking about."

"Okay," Jack nodded as I peered over his shoulder.

While Noel and Jack analyzed their commercial value, I looked at the proofs through the lens of my critical inner voice. I paused at one featuring me in a red, white and blue American flag bikini. I clutched the lapel of my leather jacket as I stared aggressively at the camera over black sunglasses that sat midway down my nose. "This could be it," I said. I was wrong.

Then it appeared. I was seated atop the Harley, clad in a white bikini, my highlighted curls falling gently on either side of my face. Despite its cheesecake factor, the image was presented in minimalism and subtlety. The absence of phony smiles and dramatic cosmetics rendered it a stark contrast to future photos I took for the website we dubbed V-TwinGirls.com. Jack's iron-fisted approach to my beauty hadn't yet taken hold. These were the simple days in for me.

"That's the one," Jack said. Noel nodded in

agreement.

"Those proofs are for you guys to keep. I'm gonna get a few posters printed of that one. I can drop them off to you next week. You guys wanna get together for lunch?"

"Sure," Jack said. "She works in Lorain County, so it's hard for her. I can meet you any day during the week, unless ya wanna wait 'til the weekend."

"No problem. I'll give you a call Monday. We'll set something up."

"Sure thing, man." Jack said as all of us shook hands.

Several days later, I came home from work to find a large tubular package on our dining room table. Jack unrolled it. The sight of myself in poster size seemed oddly daunting. Every physical feature was magnified in detail.

"I think we should frame this and take it to Rod. He'd love to have something like this hanging on the wall at Hog Heaven!" Jack gushed.

He was right. Within weeks that poster graced the bar inside Hog Heaven in Canton, where it stayed for years. Despite Jack's later admonitions urging me to cake on dark eye shadow in the name of commercial success ("I know what men like!"), my simple look made it the most popular photograph in the history of V-TwinGirls.com.

"You know," Jack said thoughtfully, "if you're going to keep doing photo shoots, or if we make a website, you need a nickname for security... sort of like a 'stage name.'"

"Hmm. I love cats," I replied, "so how 'bout Kitten?"

Kitten was christened as the chief "babe" of our unformed team, and V-TwinGirls.com.

Photo: Tumbleweed Photography

6. BIKES, BIKINIS AND BRAVERY

Confusion, this is all for the gods
Uncertainty, I could be bathing under artificial light,
Under twilight blue, starts to mesmerize
And I tell myself that you light up my life
But it's all in the mind when you cannot see in the eyes.
- DJ Tiesto, "Battleship Grey"

As days passed, Jack and I navigated the waters of married life, settling into a daily rhythm. Despite exhaustion, we remained mostly pleasant with each other during the first few months. Although we worked eight-hour days, my commute tacked on two and a half more hours to my shift, leaving me with precious little time for household chores during the work week. Yet I managed to do some laundry on these tired nights, often tossing a load of whites into the washer before dashing downstairs for a workout. Jack, on the other hand, assumed the bulk of culinary and lawn care responsibilities. The latter usually involved nearly two days of mowing the property, the acreage of which remained an ongoing mystery, depending on whatever number Jack threw out. The weekend brought more time for me to vacuum, launder, and shop for groceries.

While later months brought Jack's admonitions that chores were unevenly divided ("I do *everything* around here!"), I was nevertheless frustrated by the iron grip he held over two regions: the yard and the kitchen. The massive control he exercised in these areas was matched only by the expertise to which he laid claim. His youthful experience cooking for his father's restaurant and superior ability to fit the dimensions of the seated lawn mower rendered him the authority in these activities.

Despite his undeniable culinary abilities, my creative side yearned to blend ingredients and produce dishes with equal fervor. He touted the superiority of his talents, often comparing it to that of ex-wife Theresa, who he claimed cooked bland dishes out of boxes. "At least at my house they get a home cooked meal!" he proclaimed.

To the untrained eye, my desire to participate reflected a haphazard disregard for a buried treasure: a husband who cooks. Should I not be grateful for such a rare find? Not when it Jack's self-proclaimed superiority served as a battering ram. It's unlikely an outside observer would take pleasure enduring the watchful eye of a spouse standing in the doorway, with condescending snickers and "helpful" suggestions hurled at rapid fire pace. My unfamiliarity with his appliances and heat settings legitimized jabs at my incompetence, many of which were witnessed by his young children, who chuckled in unison with their father. Absent fish sticks and pre-packaged pasta sauce, the meals I cooked during our three year marriage can be counted on one hand.

The same can be said for lawn care. Despite the fact that I'd never operated a lawn mower, I expressed confidence that I could do so with ease.

"Why don't you show me right now? That way I could complete the back yard while you ride the seated mower in the front. C'mon. It can't be that hard!"

"It's not hard at all," Jack said. "It's just bulky. Besides, I can't envision you pushing a mower anyway."

"Well then, try to envision me on the seated mower. Take a cue from New Age folks. Meditate and visualize me there," I said, trying to inject humor into our exchange. "Seriously. Give me the key, show me how to work the controls, and I'm good to go."

"No way," he shook his head. "That mower's too big for you. Your legs wouldn't even touch the sides."

"It's big, but not *that* big," I scoffed. "Let's go out right now and see," I challenged. "You know, you could save yourself a lot of work if we mowed the property as a team."

"We *are* a team," he protested. "Don't worry about this outdoor junk," he said impatiently. "You handle the indoors and I'll handle the outdoors. How 'bout that?"

"Well alright," I shrugged. "But I don't wanna hear about the long hours you toil on the lawn, while I'm doing the 'easy stuff' inside."

And yet that's exactly what happened. If I heard this complaint once, I heard it a thousand times. "I do everything around here" became the mantra of his domestic martyrdom during tirades about my perceived laziness. It became a truism not only in his mind, but in the minds of family members who became an audience for this misinformation campaign, including Jack Jr., the kids, Theresa, and anyone else who'd listen. I morphed from an obsessive pregnant stripper into a narcissistic bikini-clad bimbo who preferred a treadmill and cosmetics to real housework.

It was only a few days following my first photo shoot with Noel when I noticed an important calendar date looming on the horizon.

"Have you thought about what you want for your birthday?" I asked Jack.

"I don't want anything for my birthday. Don't make any special plans, either. I don't really like birthdays, especially my own," he said.

Like a mischievous toddler, I began planning my rebellion against his prohibition on celebratory glee. I carefully selected a gift that suited his interest: the book "American Soldier" by General Tommy Franks. Since Gen. Franks served as the commander in chief of the U.S. Central Command in Afghanistan and Iraq, I figured his memoirs would strike a chord with Jack's purported participation in the war on terrorism. I inscribed a loving birthday wish on the inside cover, saluting Jack as my own American hero. On August 23, I took an hour of vacation time so I could arrive home early from work for my stealthy exercise. I hanged streamers and balloons with the speed of lightning. I laid Franks' book on the dining room table, along with his card.

Jack's face lit up when he walked through the door with Jenna and Jason.

"What are the balloons for?" Jill asked.

"It's your dad's birthday," I said, smiling broadly.

"Oh!" she exclaimed. "Happy birthday, Daddy!" she said, as she ran over to hug her father. Jason quickly followed suit.

"Thank you, honey. I told you not to do that," Jack chided, as he leafed through his new book with interest.

Birthday wishes quickly turned to talk of bikinis in the coming days as Jack's idea for a biker swimwear team took shape. Jack and I met a couple young women who joined me as we became the initial trio of that graced V-TwinGirls.com. The first of these was Holly, a 5'9" twenty-something blonde whose experience in local modeling and belly dance instruction rendered her a valuable asset during preparation for our Christmas debut appearance. Her size was a sticking point for Jack, for the fact she filled out a size medium sweat pant made him shiver with revulsion. However, his disgust was surpassed by the admiration he held for her ability to present herself well in front of the camera. Twisting her body with ease, she knew her most flattering angles presented and which cosmetics gave her "the look." Jack eventually tried to get me to replicate her black eye liner on my own face as he urged me to hold my head in the same manner as her poses.

"Why don't you try something for me?" he asked one day. "Sometime later, maybe this weekend when we go out, try lining your eyes a bit heavier than normal.

Sorta like Holly. I just wanna see how it looks. Could be something to do for photos, if it looks good."

"I dunno," I hesitated. "I've got ten years on her. Women have to watch lining their eyes too heavily as they age. Makes us look hard. Besides....whaddya mean, 'if it looks good?' I already look good," I said pointedly, my disappointment rising at his insinuation.

"Of course you look good," he declared. "Don't be silly. It's just a suggestion, so don't get defensive! If we're gonna keep doing this stuff, you have to be able to handle constructive criticism. You can learn from Holly's experience. See?" he said, as he scrolling to one of her pictures. "You should also get some silver hoop earrings like that. They look great with leather."

"I can see learning from her posing skill, but I can't see copying her look," I replied thoughtfully. At that point in our marriage, I had enough spunk to call a spade a spade, albeit in a calm voice. "I'm disturbed by your tone, Jack. If you're gonna assume a position of providing 'constructive criticism' to your wife, I need to point something out on my own. Any make-up artist from Hollywood to New York will say the same make-up can't be applied to two women with different hair colors and skin tones. Holly's golden blonde and fair skinned. I'm tan and I've got dark brown hair with a few highlights. Is this computing?"

"'I'm disturbed by your tone, Jack,'" he mimicked. "You're taking this all wrong," he said with a sigh. "You're turning my words against me and blowing a simple suggestion out of proportion. Yeah, this is just a hobby, but it could turn into something more for you. I'm not trying to get you to 'copy' her look, I'm just..... Oh never mind. Ya know what? I'm gonna shut up. Do whatever you want." He turned away, and faced the computer screen.

With a few brief sentences I punctured his

authoritative stance and flawed reasoning, both of which insulted his ego. He didn't anticipate that his new wife would meet his suggestion with resistance, so he backed off our conversation. It was the first time he attempted to engineer a change in me, but it wasn't the last. Those were the early days of our dysfunction, when I resisted his efforts to recreate my image and when he withdrew instead of shouting. Jack eventually understood that he had to widen his tactical range to secure my capitulation.

When the weekend arrived, I decided to try something new. As we prepared to eat out, I applied my eyeliner with a slightly heavier stroke than normal. I wondered if Jack would notice my willingness to try his suggestion. He did.

Just as we walked out the door, Jack turned to kiss me. As he backed away, he cocked his head and squinted at my face.

"You did something different with your makeup. You added more liner, didn't you?"

"A bit," I said, as I scanned his face for approval.

"Nice," he smiled. "Not that you didn't look good before. It's just different. I like it

By altering my makeup, I was attempting to show Jack that I could accept his suggestion, but not with unquestioning obedience. When he withdrew from discussion days before, I made my point. Now I wanted to display my openness to his point of view. But my behavior actually taught him that I was malleable. The stage was set. And the worst was yet to come.

As autumn rust leaves fell onto our grass, a medical mystery fell into our lives. One brisk October night, I awoke to Jack's pained groan.

"Oh! Oh! Oh...god." I rolled over to find him clutching his shoulder in apparent agony.

"What's wrong, hon?" I asked frantically.

"My shoulder's killing me!" he exclaimed. "I can't

move it. I don't know what's wrong. I'm scared. This has never happened before."

"Does it feel like you slept on it wrong?" I asked.

"No! I can't move it at all." At my urging, we Jack donned his jeans and we headed to the emergency room.

As we walked into the night air, I noticed a sight that nearly stopped me dead in my tracks. Out of the corner of my right eye I saw mist rising from our pond encased in the lunar glow of a moon that appeared full. It was an inconvenient moment for me to be caught up by Mother Nature's beauty, but the eerie display left me awestruck. I couldn't help but survey the wondrous scene as I fumbled for my car keys. "Wow," I whispered. I wanted to approach the pond and envelop myself in the mist, but the urgency of our situation beckoned.

"Just direct me to the hospital," I said.

Once we were inside the examining room, Jack faced a barrage of questions. "Any prior surgeries?"

Following a pregnant pause, he finally replied, "Yeah...it was a long time ago." He still clutched his shoulder.

"In what anatomical region?"

"I was in the military," he declared. "Got shot a few times. Once in the lung, the other in my thigh. Back in the eighties."

"Okay," the doctor replied without further inquiry.

Neither the ER physician nor any subsequent diagnostic test determined the cause of Jack's distress. Although I shelled out money for a couple months of temporary health insurance for him, numerous visits to a variety of doctors' offices failed to shed light on the source of his shoulder's meltdown. While I accompanied him on a couple of the early appointments, I remained on duty at court when his final encounter with a doctor occurred.

"How did it go at the doctor's?" I immediately asked after I came through the door. "What did he say?"

"Ah, I don't know. It wasn't worth it," he said, sitting down to the computer.

"What do ya mean, ya don't know what he said?" I queried.

"They just don't know!" he snapped. "The doctor said it might be a viral infection in my muscle that I picked up in South America somewhere. Who the hell knows?"

The mystery behind Jack's pain continued longer than the pain itself. In the weeks that followed that fateful ER visit, he reported being plagued with pain on a regular basis. Sometimes it subsided with my massage, he explained, but it usually came and went.

"My body's falling apart, Melissa," he said solemnly the following week. "It's been through so much and I've treated it like crap. This is my body's revenge. It's giving out on me."

Days later, our photographer came to the rescue with painkillers that provided a temporary balm to Jack's aches and pains. Once Noel heard Jack's story, he donated a few prescription medications that saw him through pain brought about by an auto accident the previous year.

"Now Jack, you gotta watch how you do this. You can't take these things during the day," Noel warned. "Only take 'em at night."

Despite the repeated misgivings Jack expressed to me about taking someone else's prescription medication, he awoke with relief the first morning after taking the meds.

"That was the first restful night of sleep I've had in weeks!" Jack explained.

One chilly November weeknight, Jack expressed a desire to eat out. "Let's go to Hog Heaven and grab a bite to eat," he said. "This shoulder's been getting me down; I need to get out of the house."

We walked into our county's version of Cheers, the barbeque restaurant where "everyone knew our name." Or, at least, they knew my picture that graced the bar. Staff greeted us with warm greetings.

Following our pork sandwiches, I excused myself to the ladies' room. "I'll be right back, hon." I made my way through the second dining area, where the restrooms were found near the rear wall. After addressing the call of nature, I washed my hands and exited. As I re-entered the main dining room, I saw a couple of gentlemen seated at a table, one of whom looked strikingly familiar. The resemblance suddenly occurred to me. The gentleman on the left appeared to be Richard, an employee of the detention facilities at my juvenile court. As he looked up from his plate, I smiled and nodded politely. As I prepared to stop at their table, I realized my mistake. The fellow was a bit too hefty to be Richard, so I continued to my seat at the bar. As I approached Jack, I noticed him glowering at me over his bottle of Rolling Rock.

"I'm disappointed," he said, peeling the label from his bottle.

"Disappointed in what?" I asked.

He stared at me, his steely blue eyes blazing with an anger I'd never seen before.

"You're a horrible liar," he declared, as he called to the barmaid for our check.

I paused for a few moments, reeling from his verbal missile. Finally I found the words to speak. "What do you mean?" I asked.

"You *know* what I mean," he said aside to me in a low voice, as he paid our check. "I'm not discussing it here."

"Well, you're sure willing to label me here," I said with bewilderment. I shrugged. "Don't see why you'd stop there."

I followed Jack out the door into the parking lot. The air was thick with tension as he started the car. It became apparent with each passing moment that he wasn't going to discuss the reasons behind his accusatory barb. It's possible he was waiting for me to unleash dramatically righteous indignation, but that wasn't my style. I figured that he'd talk when he was ready. Finally I broke the icy silence with a feeble attempt at small talk.

"It's funny," I said, motioning backward towards the restaurant. "I actually thought I recognized an employee from the court in there tonight. Good thing it wasn't him. Could've been awkward explaining my poster behind the bar," I snickered.

"That's a horrible save!" Jack declared.

"Okay," I said finally, "are you gonna tell me the reason for your mood, or do I have to play guessing games? Whatever's up here, we need to talk about it like adults."

"You know," he said slowly, "I've never even looked at another woman since I started dating you. You crushed me tonight. I watched you return from the restroom and observed your interaction with that guy, and I couldn't believe my eyes, Melissa." Had I known the true nature of his relationship with Linda, I would've hit him between his hypocritical eyes. Sure, he never *looked* at another woman since our courtship; he just two-timed me and screwed his girlfriend following our ceremony. I fumbled mentally through the list of possible "guys" to which he referred.

"The only guys I remember were the ones sitting at a table near the wall. The dude on the left was the one I just mentioned. I was getting ready to stop , but I realized it wasn't him..."

"Just save it," he interjected. "I've been trained to

read people, to watch their body language, to gauge their mental state from their eyes. I've had to determine threat levels when I walked in a room. Do you understand what I'm saying?" He turned from the steering wheel.

"Yeah...that you've been trained to look for threats," I said. My guts churned as I realized the direction Jack was taking. His military education aside, I had some training of my own. The five years I spent advocating for a domestic violence shelter familiarized me with numerous stories of possessive men projecting insecurities onto their mates. This wasn't good, and I knew it had to be nipped in the bud. Perhaps I could prompt him into self-analysis with calm reason. "Since you're trained to look for threats in a life-or-death context and you've seen too many to mention," I continued, "do you think it's possible that you anticipate them when they don't exist? Not because you try to, but maybe in the old survival mode?"

"Don't put this back on me!" he said, his voice rising. "There's a specific look that people have when they see something that scares, or pleases, them. Their pupils dilate, their heart rate increases. It's the classic predator response to seeing something that's desired... for prey or sexual opportunity."

"Predator?" I asked incredulously. I would've exploded in spasms of laughter had the moment not been so serious. "I've definitely heard of the fight-or-flight mechanism," I said, my own soul yearning for flight at that very moment! "I've just never heard a 'predator' label applied to a scenario involving facial recognition of a colleague. It doesn't wash."

"Melissa, you can say whatever you want. I saw those guys look up at you. One of them smiled. You smiled in acknowledgment. As you passed their table, he turned back to his buddy."

"Makes sense to me," I said as we rolled into our

driveway. "That has a way of happening between two friends. They have a tendency to focus on their own conversation, ya know?" My exasperation was beginning to show.

"Give me a break, alright?" he said, as we entered the house. He opened the sliding door to let Minnie out. I flopped on the sofa, shaking my head in anticipation of his next missile. He was too keyed up to stop. I sighed, shaking my head.

"Go ahead and sigh!" he shouted. "Sorry to bore you with my concerns." Within moments, Minnie re-appeared and he let her in. Turning, he began a bizarre interrogation. "So you're telling me you actually *believe* an employee from Lorain County would be eating at a Canton restaurant? Puh-LEEZE!"

"Yes, I'm telling you that. One of the employees was sitting right beside you all evening. She's sitting right here in front of you, too. I thought you knew her pretty well, but now that she's the target of your misplaced anger, I'm not so sure."

"There's a difference between eating near your house, and choosing to dine at a restaurant over an hour away! There's no reason why a person from there would come all the way to Canton just to eat dinner." Jack rolled his eyes. "You're just trying to put a good spin on this 'cause I caught you flirting."

"This may surprise you," I said slowly, "but several of our employees own motorcycles and ride all over Northeast Ohio. Some of their children in high school athletics often compete with teams from Stark County schools. Being a former football player at Perry High, I'm sure you already knew that. Lorain County is only an hour away. It's not the other side of the world, Jack."

My veiled anger didn't produce the return volley he wanted, a fact that enraged him. "You refuse to admit it, don't ya?" he demanded, pacing like a caged animal. "I worship you, Melissa. I adore you. Here I am, a husband who's secure enough to let his wife pose in a bikini and be looked at by other guys. Then you violate my trust. What were you doing... culling your catch? Looking to see if others are out there?"

"If I was attempting that, I wouldn't be sitting here, Jack. Judging from tonight, I don't think you're as secure with this 'Kitten' thing as you let on. This isn't the mark of confidence. As a matter of fact, many counselors from my old shelter would say it's the mark of something much worse." I struck a nerve.

"Oh so you think I'm going to turn into some controlling abuser?"

"Well," I said, "you tell me, Jack. This is out of character for you. You never pulled this accusatory crap when we dated, or when we went out with my male colleagues. When it suddenly emerges like this, I gotta wonder where it's leading." I lowered my voice and patted the floor. "Have a seat. I know you're going through a rough time right now, hon... and maybe this shoulder problem is playing tricks with your self-esteem. But that doesn't mean I deserve the insecurity you're throwing my way. This isn't right."

The more I tried to reason, the angrier he became. Even I was unprepared for the unvarnished insult he hurled next. With a roll of his eyes, he rolled out a verbal bullet that pierced my heart and irretrievably damaged our young marriage.

"Go ahead and admit it. If I hadn't been there, you would've fucked him!"

I couldn't believe my ears. "You're serious?" I asked. "You're really serious?"

"If I wasn't there, you would've indulged that attraction."

With that, I rose from the sofa. "That's it," I said.

"This isn't right, it's not justified, and it's not healthy. If you believe that, you don't need to be married to me. I'm not gonna be an audience for this crap. When you're ready to discuss this like a civilized adult, fine. I'm taking a shower."

Upon seeing me leave, Jack softened his tone. "It's not that I don't wanna be married to you," he called out.

"Of course not," I said. "You wanna be married to me. You just want the luxury of using me as a lightning rod for your manly insecurities. That ain't gonna happen." Eventually did, and it worsened. For the time being, though, Jack appeared to back off.

"Okay, maybe it was unfair to say you would've fucked him."

"*Maybe* it was unfair? Maybe?"

"All I ask is be patient with me," he pleaded. "Maybe you're right about my self-esteem lately. Please... please... don't overreact to this. We're a new couple. Couples argue. Maybe your parents didn't argue much, but it's perfectly normal," he rationalized.

"Don't pass this off as healthy conflict," I said. "My parents may have argued, but they never cursed or accused each other of baloney like this. If you think this is okay, you need help."

"So now you think I'm crazy?"

"I said, 'If you think this is okay, you need help.' Period. I'll be out of the shower in a bit." I walked up the stairs.

I reached for my makeup remover and dabbed my eyes, amazed at their lack of tears. I took off my clothes mechanically, replaying the night's scene in my mind. I pulled back the shower curtain with fingers that twitched with anxiety. I climbed into my cubicle of refuge and took a deep breath as the cool water slowed my adrenaline and washed the pain away. Maybe this was an isolated outburst, I told myself. Maybe his good will would prevail. Water dripped from my hands as I reached for a brown towel that resonated with memories of home. I ran my hands over the cross stitched pattern Mom had created as I thought of the respect my parents held for one another, a respect I thought I'd found with Jack. My eyes began to sting as I cried into the cloth. After a couple minutes, I dried off and donned my bedclothes.

I walked into the bedroom to find Jack preparing for bed. I checked the alarm clock before climbing under the covers. Within seconds he snuggled up to spoon with me, and reached his hand to cup my right breast.

"Honey," I said, "maybe we can do this another time. I'm really tired and emotionally exhausted. Let's create some special time tomorrow."

"Are you still mad about what I said?" he asked.

"Not mad as much as exhausted," I sighed. "And yes, some things remain unresolved for me. But that doesn't mean everything's gonna be perfect tonight. Let's get some sleep."

"It would mean a lot to me if we could make love," he said. "That's all."

"Just a few minutes ago, you declared I'd perform the same act with another man. I'm having a hard time responding. Right now, I want to rest."

"Well, no matter how mad I get," he said with his arm still around me. "I'll never hold myself back from you."

"Please," he persisted, "it would mean a lot to me."

I rolled over and silently acquiesced to his advances. I neither sought nor received any pleasure from the act. It was comfort I wanted, and it was comfort I received, however temporary. I was grateful when sleep arrived to rescue me from the disquieting thoughts racing through my head. Little did I know, it would not be the last time I prayed for slumber to be my savior.

Slumber was the last thing on my mind as the next few weeks brought increased preparations for the debut of our fledgling V-Twin Girl trio. Jack and Noel rolled out life-size posters of each of us. My eyes widened as Jack held up a large version of me clad in leather.

"We're gonna hang these at Pancho's Basement a couple weeks before you guys make your appearance. That way, all Steve's customers can see you'll be there in December. There's still planning to do, though. We have to think of what each of you will do for a talent routine. It's nice to have pretty girls, but we should give his audience a bit more. You come out dancing as a group at first, then we add a few intermissions for product giveaways. If each of you does one 4-5 minute talent routine of some kind, it'll work out to be half an hour. That works."

"Speaking of Steve, are we receiving anything for our efforts, or is this a freebie to get him to invite us back?"

"He's throwing us a bone and giving us a buck for each paid admission that night. We'll just let the girls split it. It's no profit for us, 'cause I figure your share helps us pay some expenses. If all goes well, we'll ask for more next time. I think that's a good route to take right now."

"Uh-huh," I said, leafing through the mail. "So about this talent thing... I don't sing or dance. Shall I get up and recite the Bill of Rights?"

"You've sung before, haven't you?"

"Not unless you count freshman choir. The only thing I can think of would be to sing *without singing*, sort of in a breathy whisper.... like Marilyn Monroe did when she sang "Happy Birthday" to the president. Maybe I could manage that."

"Alright," he nodded. "What would you sing, or whisper?"

"It's the holiday season, so something Christmas. How 'bout 'Santa Baby?'"

"Sounds good. We'll download the lyrics so you can start memorizing them."

"I'm not so sure about this, though," I hesitated. "Singing's not my thing. Besides, this goes beyond picture taking. We're a fledgling bikini team, not 'American Idol.'"

"We're just getting started," he said impatiently. "You have to use common sense! We can't just parade unknown girls in bikinis in front of an audience, without doing something to get them interested. Holly can do her belly dancing, Sheri can dance to a hip-hop routine. You've gotta have some kind of talent, especially as our team leader. Can't just prance out and say, 'Hi, I'm a cute attorney.' That will turn 'em off. You need something else. 'Santa Baby' will work."

For the next month, Eartha Kitt and Madonna serenaded me during my health and beauty regimens with renditions of "Santa Baby." Since Kitt's rendition contained an easier rhythm for me, I asked Jack to download a slower karaoke version. It was no small feat, but he finally found "the one" that became my signature tune.

My preparation for Kitten's singing debut was offset by the excitement I felt as Thanksgiving approached. Not only was it the first major holiday Jack and I shared, but it marked my parents' first visit to our marital home. This gave my beloved a chance to showcase his culinary skills, a chore he secretly relished despite complaints about his titanic efforts, shoulder pain, or the oversight I showed at failing to secure all the correct ingredients at the store. When he showed off his strengths, he felt secure. When he was secure, he was happy. And when he was happy, our home wasn't plagued with stress.

I paced in and out of the living room, waiting for their car to roll into the driveway. As I returned to the den to watch the ever-present Fox News channel (the only acceptable news outlet in Jack's world), I heard Minnie bark. Then the doorbell rang. I rose excitedly. When I opened the door, I hugged my parents hello.

"Something smells awfully good in here," Mom said as they walked into the kitchen where my husband was practicing his artistry. All of us exchanged hugs and sat down to a wonderful meal. Since Jack Jr. was in town, his presence at the dinner table was an unexpected treat. Afterwards, we retired to the den for several hours of conversation peppered with Jack's usual military references. This provided a perfect opportunity for my animal-loving parents to become acquainted with our blended family of pets. As Jack rough-housed with Minnie, elderly Sammie activated his feline charm as Mom petted him into a steady purr.

"Wow," she said, "he's so thin."

"Yeah," Jack said as he broke from his wrestling match with the dog. "He's always been a lean cat. He's old, but he keeps Melissa's young'un Artie on her toes."

"Speaking of Artie," she said, peering around for the gray tiger-striped face.

"She'll come out in a while," I said. "Probably hiding from the holiday commotion."

"No doubt," Jack said. "Talk about a skittish cat! I started calling her 'Tweak', after that character on 'South Park.'"

Minnie ventured from the floor mat where she lay to greet my parents. Mom petted her golden fur. "Is she allowed on the sofa?"

"No!" Jack said firmly. "It's a pain to clean all that fur off the fabric. We vacuum constantly in here as it is."

I hated for the night to end. Eventually I faced reality as we ventured upstairs and my parents made their way to Jenna's room, which served as their temporary guest quarters. They weren't gone yet, and I already missed them. When we bid goodbye the following day, I was happy we were already talking about Christmas.

"Come on back next month," Jack said. "I'll have to work something out with the kids' mom. They'll probably be over Christmas morning. We'd love to have you back!"

I wistfully watched my parents leave as I turned around and wandered into the den. As Jack trotted into the office to work on our computer, I tried to distract myself with various cable channels as my thoughts trailed to Christmas. I rose from the sofa.

"Hey hon," I called out, "I'm gonna go downstairs and hop on the treadmill."

"Okay," he said absentmindedly, staring at the computer screen. "The Pancho's appearance is coming up soon. Might wanna take that 'Santa Baby' CD downstairs with you downstairs and practice."

"It's not workout music. I'm going downstairs to exercise, not practice. I can do that later."

"Well ya don't have a hell of a lot of time. I think it would be a good idea if you rehearsed it in front of me tomorrow night, maybe after your workout."

"I don't understand," I said. "Why?"

"I wanna make sure you're gonna pull this off. I don't think you're taking it seriously." I opened the basement door. "So you're just walking away, huh?"

"I'm doing the exercising I set out to do, hon," I replied. "And I don't see a need to rehearse in front of you. It's not like you're calling any of the *other* girls over for a rehearsal of *their* routines. I can understand with Holly, 'cause she's experienced in her belly dancing. But

Sheri isn't, and you haven't asked for a rehearsal of her freestyle dance routine."

"Whatever," he said. "Fine... just go downstairs."

After days of preparation and memorization that included one private performance for Jack, the day finally arrived. Off we went to the small town of New Philadelphia for our trio's debut at Pancho's Basement. The smell of Mexican cuisine greeted us as we entered the upper floor. We strolled downstairs past the life-size posters to our dressing room, where we performed several clothing changes throughout the evening. Midway through our show, I donned my red velveteen mini-dress and Santa cap and slinked onto the stage, where I performed "Santa Baby" with flawlessly memorized lyrics. Not only was the audience receptive, but even Jack himself later complimented my performance.

The overall success of our evening was marred by a revelation the two women made to me in the privacy of our dressing room. Holly and Sherri reported that they'd been the subject of Noel's advances, describing in detail how the photographer asked them out on dates and commented on their personal lives. After I summoned Jack into the room, we assured the women that from that moment on, we would always be present at photo shoots involving Noel. We also assured them that we intended to seek services from another photographer as soon as possible.

On our way home, Jack declared confidently that he could do the photography with equal skill with some well-chosen equipment. "You know," he said, "with the right camera, I could do just as well as Noel. And we wouldn't have the headache of our photographer hitting on the girls."

"Are you sure about that? Not that I don't think you're talented, but it's a lot of work."

"I used to snap photos all the time when I did nature features for the paper," he said. "Noel's got a good eye for some things, but he gets the lighting level wrong a lot. I gotta edit his photos constantly. Let's start scouting out 35 mm cameras on eBay this week and see what kind of deals are out there."

"I think we should hold off for now," I said. "Christmas is coming, and we need to get some gifts for the family. We're barely making our bills as it is."

"This is more important!" he declared with a fervor that demonstrated an appallingly skewed sense of priorities.

"Please tell me you didn't mean that photographing bikes and babes is more important than creating a nice holiday for your family. Just assure me of that....please?"

"It's all about money," he sighed with exasperation. "Christmas is all about buying things now. Buy, buy, buy."

"Don't turn this into a commentary about holiday commercialism. This is about having priorities on a limited budget. In my eyes, family comes first. I always thought you felt the same way. Am I right?"

"Yeah, I guess so," he said half-heartedly.

"We also have the Alltel bill to pay off. Remember when you got upset when I reminded you about the allotted minutes? You said 'I need to!' and "This is more important' then, too. Our combined cells went to over three hundred dollars, all for the sake of the V-Twin Girls. When that expense is paid off, maybe we can think about the next purchase for V-Twin."

I might as well have talked to a wall. "There's always bills. We've just *got* to find a way to get a camera. That's all there is to it!" We eventually purchased the camera of his dreams in February, only to be met with expenses for lights (eighty dollars), white cloth for a photographic background, fees for numerous photo developments, a digital camera that surpassed the 35mm (one hundred forty dollars), and a never-ending list of items that increased with his frustration level. "If I only had.. [insert random supply item].. I could produce quality photos" was his battle cry.

As the holiday approached, I wanted to learn more of my blended family's traditions so that I could ensure a smooth transition for Jason and Jenna. I asked Jack how they normally observed the holiday. He explained that he normally went to their house Christmas morning.

"I watch the kids open gifts, sometimes eat brunch, then I come back here. I gotta call Theresa and figure out how she wants to handle it this year."

Within days, Jack and Theresa determined a compromise in which the kids would divide their time between our homes. I got excited as the holiday approached. More than ever, I was happy to see my parents as they joined me in celebrating my first Christmas as Jack's wife.

My parents lounged in our den as Jack bustled about preparing his hallmark table spread and enlisting my assistance in our kitchen. "Spoon these potatoes out as I hold the bowl," he said. His levels of tension and condescension increased loudly as he began to berate me for not moving certain dishes out of his way, not setting out food items at his preferred pace, and a host of other irritations. Jack Jr. had dismissed his dad's behavior during Thanksgiving preparation with a wry smile and "Yeah, that's normal." However, I was unwilling to let his performance continue before this audience. I was certain his tirade was overheard by my parents, whose opinions of Jack I sadly valued above my own treatment. My eyes stinging with humiliation, I leaned over the kitchen counter and summoned Jack over with a loud whisper.

"What?!?" he turned impatiently towards me.

"Come here a sec," I hissed. I pointed at him in one of the firmest statements I made in our entire marriage. "Don't you ever, *ever*, **ever** talk to me that way, especially in front of my parents! They heard you. If you can't talk to me respectfully, cook in silence! It's less embarrassing."

"Okay," Jack sighed without apology, casting a furtive glance in the direction of the den.

"You guys need any help?" I heard my mother call out.

"Nah, that's okay," Jack said, rolling his eyes.

"Besides," I raised my voice, "you guys are guests anyway."

The holiday saw both good-natured celebration, as well as a protracted discussion about Jack's military history. Just as he began to discuss one of his purported missions, he stopped.

"I don't know if I should go on. There's something I've never told you. Melissa's the only person that knows, aside from my SEAL team mates. I don't know you guys very well, but I feel like I can trust you."

After we encouraged his catharsis, he spilled forth a horrific tale of murder and mayhem that arose during a mission in Nicaragua. His voice trembled as he described how his team came upon a grisly scene of a young girl who'd been raped and murdered by Sandinista forces for talking with Americans. With minimal investigation, his team eventually found the culprits.

"I knew what I had to do," he said solemnly. "I told my team mates to get out. I didn't want them involved or blamed for my decision."

He described the manner in which he dispatched the men, each of which he bound and executed with precision.

"I had them kneel, and I shot each of them in the back of the head."

The ensuing military investigation led to his arrest, he explained, as he described how his admiral saved him from the clutches of a full-fledged court martial with a few well-chosen lies.

"I was demoted a couple ranks, down to an E4 and I learned to live with it. The memories never left, though," he said, sighing deeply. "And I've always lived with the fear that the case could be re-opened. All it takes is for one determined reporter to file an inquiry under the Freedom of Information Act and I could go to prison."

My parents and I discussed various coping mechanisms for the horrific memories that plagued his tortured soul. We had no way of knowing that the true torture wasn't inflicted upon Jack, but *by* him- or rather, his dishonesty. And we certainly didn't realize the joke was on us.

My parents were treated to several dubious goodies during their holiday visit. Aside from being regaled with Jack's tale of vengeful bravery, they also observed unnerving interactions with me and the animal members of our household. Mom looked on with silent concern at Jack's rough-housing with the pets, fearful she might alienate me if she criticized my new husband. My parents' perception of Jack wasn't helped by his blasé willingness to demonstrate a military killing technique on me at the dining room table. They watched aghast as he grabbed my neck in a choke hold as if to snap it.

As Jack and I lay in bed that night, he seemed to look forward to his houseguests' departure. "Don't get me wrong, I love your parents," he said. "I just like our time together too. Does that make sense?"

"Yeah," I said. "I just don't get to see them very often now."

The day following Christmas, my mom's mind buzzed with silent fears. Once again I watched in sadness as my parents walked out the door. Despite the fact our domestic trouble was in its infancy, a knot was forming in my gut. I instinctively knew my only source of genuine support was leaving our driveway. I was right.

As they made their way down the highway, Mom issued an ominously prophetic observation about Jack and me: "I don't think this marriage is going to last."

7. THE DESCENT

I try to blame it on fortune, some kind of twist in my fate.
I know the truth and it haunts me.
I learned it a little too late.
- Sir Elton John and Janet Jackson, "I Know the Truth"

Beep! Beep! The alarm clock brutally sliced through my consciousness. It was my first day returning to work following Christmas. More importantly, December 27 was my mother's birthday. As I donned my suit I thanked myself that we'd found time to observe her special day during my parents' holiday visit. I summoned all the motivation I could muster and drove to Elyria, where I commenced my first round of child support hearings. Shortly before lunchtime the phone rang. I paused to look at the caller identification panel. It was Jack, calling from the radio station.

"I don't know what's going on," he blurted in a panic-stricken voice.

"What's wrong?"

"I don't know!" he exclaimed. "I came back from meeting with a client and found this paper left for me. The sheriff delivered it. It says I've gotta pick up something. Oh God!"

"Read it to me, if you can," I replied. "Is there a case number on there you can look up?"

"There's a number, yeah. But I don't have my own computer here, and I sure as hell ain't gonna use one of the sales rep's terminals. I don't want them knowing my business!"

"Hold on. I'm gonna close my office door," I said. I returned to my desk and logged onto the internet, where I navigated to the Stark County government's website. "Okay, tell me the number."

My eyes widened as the case docket

downloaded. "Linda's suing you," I said flatly.

"Suing me? For *what*?"

"It's probably about the money you owe her."

"But I've been paying her $150 every month! What else does she want from me?"

"Yes," I replied, "we've been faithfully issuing her a monthly check out of our joint checking account, but it's less than the original $200 you and she discussed. Even you told me that, Jack."

"But she told me it would be okay to pay less until I got on my feet!" he protested.

"Well," I said, "we don't have all the facts yet. Just pick it up as soon as you can, and I'll look at it when I get home from work. Whatever you do, don't call her to protest. She's obviously pissed enough to sue. You have to pick up the summons."

"Hell with that bitch! I ain't picking up nothing!"

"It's too late, Jack. You've been provided notice at your employer that the summons awaits. It would be impossible for you to deny it when the your station's receptionist handed the notice to you. Bite the bullet, pick it up, and we'll talk at home."

I arrived home to find Jack pacing the floor like a caged animal. "How could she do this to me?" he muttered. I sank into the sofa as I read the documents that constituted my first major wake-up call during our marriage. I stared at my husband in silent rage.

"What's that look for?" he demanded.

"She's suing you for $24,000, Jack," I said in a carefully controlled monotone. "It's three times the 'eight to ten thousand' you originally claimed to owe her."

"Look, I *told* you she leant me some money in hard times. I told you it was a lot, too."

"Yes," I replied, "and when you said 'eight to ten thousand,' I thought that was definitely a lot of money. This is $24,000."

"Ten, twenty, twenty-four.... I'm not good with numbers, alright?"

"You remember your SEAL team number, your BUDS graduation class, the amount of kills you have in the SEAL program, your ex-wife's birthday, and the amount you paid for your car, all with flawless precision. But a $16,000 difference in a loan seeps through your memory," I said.

"So you think I lied to you about the money?"

"What would you think if the tables were turned?" Jack had no response. My jaw dropped as I read further.

"Okay, what *now*?"

"The $24,000 is based on a promissory note that you signed two weeks after we married... without my knowledge." Jack sighed and stared out the window as I continued. "Someone who's just married an attorney would normally want to have her look over a financial agreement of this magnitude. Unless, of course, there's a reason he doesn't want his spouse to see it."

"You know, I don't need this right now, Melissa. This is $24,000 that I don't have. I gotta figure out a way to deal with it."

"Thanks to your secret promissory note, Jack, it ain't just about you anymore. You know, some courts would consider this a marital debt."

"Oh boy," he said shaking his head absentmindedly. "I shoulda never fucked her!"

"What?" I asked in abject amazement. I hadn't been hit this hard since Jack's accusatory rant the previous month. "You told me you were strictly platonic friends."

"Huh?" he said, caught off guard. "We *were* platonic for the most part. We only had sex a handful of times."

"A handful? You told me twice during our courtship that the two of you never had sex!"

"No I didn't say that," he paused,....."did I?"

"Yep," I nodded. "How things change. Your relationship with her is no longer platonic, now it's a $24,000 debt instead of eight thousand, and the icing on the cake? There's a promissory note I never knew of. Anything else you haven't told me? Might as well get it out now."

"I'm sorry, Melissa."

"Are you sorry you lied to me, or are you sorry you got caught?" I asked.

"Don't get like that. I'm sorry for hurting you. You're all that matters to me, and I held back information you should've known."

"Held back? You didn't just 'hold back.' You lied."

"Okay, I'm **sorry**!" he said defensively. "I was only trying to protect you!"

"You protected yourself, Jack. You didn't protect me."

"Alright, alright," he said, dismissing my challenge. "I realize what I did was wrong. Now what can I do about this? *You're* the attorney."

"I'm also your wife; I shouldn't have to rescue you from something you did to her *and* me!" I sighed, cradling my head in my hands as I stared at the carpet dejectedly. While my mother observed her birthday over a hundred and fifty miles away, I was struck with a bitter irony. My parents' courtship had lasted a fraction of ours, yet their marriage contained twenty times the respect and honesty. I had little faith in my husband at that point, but I felt like I had no recourse except to stay the course. Although our stability was rocked by this controversy, it didn't constitute physical abuse or infidelity, leaving me with no justification for exiting the marriage. At least that's what I told myself, despite the gnawing feeling that our relationship wasn't right. Maybe I wasn't meant to enjoy a happy marriage, I thought. My reverie was broken by his angry plea.

"I'm sorry, but I still need your help. You just gonna sit there and let Linda drive me into the poorhouse? You gotta tell me what I can do!"

"Simply put, Jack, you signed a valid promissory note. She's got you dead to rights. You must pay her back. And this mere $150 we've been sending? She didn't agree to the reduced amount in writing, so it's hard to prove her consent unless she admits she ok'd it."

"So I'm fucked. Is that what you're saying?"

"The law is on her side, like it or not."

"You're a lawyer and you can't even help. What good are lawyers anyway?" he sputtered, as he began a rant on the uselessness of my education. It was strikingly similar to the monologue he often delivered about his sister, whose legal education was rendered "useless" by her decision to raise her kids at home. Unless it served him in some way, it seemed the education of women close to him was "useless."

"Save the indignation," I sighed. "Had you sought my input prior to signing this note, we wouldn't be in this position. I could've crafted an agreement that limited her legal remedies. But you made a choice to be secretive, and this situation is a product of that choice."

"Enough of the psycho-babble!" Jack roared. "I sure don't have the money to pay her."

"True. Neither of us do. Plus you have other bills to consider. And child support. Hate to say it, but your best legal option may be to declare bankruptcy. On a moral level, you should pay everyone, but it's impossible. On a legal level, it makes sense."

"I'm not giving up my house for that bitch! I worked too hard. I helped build this place!"

"Sounds like 'the bitch' basically paid the mortgage for this place. Well, depending on the equity you have, you'll be able to keep the property." I was unaware he'd refinanced several times, including following his divorce from Theresa and again in 2003. Equity was a non-issue. I explained the differences between Chapter 7 and Chapter 13. "With a Chapter 13 repayment, you make one monthly payment to the court. You keep your house and car while paying creditors at a reduced rate."

"Yeah!" he said sarcastically. "Great. I gotta go under just because of her. So can you represent me in the bankruptcy or what?"

"No, because I have a conflict of interest. I'm your wife."

"Great!" he sputtered again. "Fucking lawyers!"

I resigned myself to our situation and assisted Jack with his pro se response to Linda's lawsuit. It was an inauspicious beginning to our new year, a bitter omen of our impending financial ruin. In keeping with his custom of ignoring my "useless" legal advice, Jack apparently called Linda the following day. I came home from work to find him muttering angrily about her lawsuit.

"I tried to call Linda today."

"What? I told you not to do that."

"I had to. I *had* to find out why she's doing this to me. Plus I wanted to find if there was a way we could reach an agreement without going to court. She was hysterical, all over the map."

"And what did you expect by calling someone who's suing you?"

"She was ranting about what she's gonna come into court and say. She even said, 'I'll tell the judge we slept together after you and Melissa returned from Vegas.'" he claimed, throwing up his hands helplessly. "I asked, 'But why would you even say something like that, Linda?' She's so vindictive that she'll say anything!" It was his latest attempt to inoculate me from an embarrassing truth by providing his own spin before the emergence of the real story. It was a technique he employed with increasing frequency as the potential for exposure grew.

By the time Jack consulted a bankruptcy attorney in January, his temper became increasingly unpredictable and his critique of my appearance intensified. His barbs were peppered with occasional compliments paid to my "natural" look: "I may like you all made up for the V-Twin Girls, but this is how I like you best." Still, the ratio of negative to positive comments skyrocketed at an alarming rate.

As more ladies entered our revolving V-Twin Girl door, Jack determined that he wanted to transform the team from biker bikini models to a performance troupe. This brainchild was spawned when his attention was captured by a Los Angeles-based group of women called the "Purrfect Angelz," whose website featured shapely dancers, singers, and acrobats that touted experience as NFL cheerleaders and models for major magazines. I walked into the computer room and looked at the screen where he was pointing to glitzy multimedia graphics.

"Check this out. This group travels all over the country to trade shows and biker events. They produce merchandise, sell calendars, and they've got a huge fan base. And on top of it all, they're hot! We can do this, and we can do it better."

"That's a cool website," I said. "It's a far cry from a biker bikini team, don't ya think?"

"Yeah, but there's nothing wrong with dreaming big, right? C'mon, I'm starting to think you don't care about this. And you're the one whose picture started it all."

"I'm just saying that we didn't begin with this concept, and maybe that's a good thing, given that we're in Stark County, Ohio."

"What d'ya mean?" he asked. "This is what I want!" he demanded petulantly, pointing to the computer screen. "Maybe not the acrobatics, but we can do the rest."

"It's not just the acrobatics, hon. Dreaming is good, but so is realism. After all, I dreamed of becoming an attorney but I was realistic. My GPA wasn't going to get me into Harvard or Columbia, so I fulfilled my dream at an Ohio law school. I succeeded because I worked within, rather than denied, my limitations. Had I banged my head up against a wall with an all-or-nothing approach, I never would've become an attorney."

"You're not very driven, are you?"

"You didn't hear me. If you're not going to listen to what I say, Jack, please don't call me in and ask what I think."

This became a perpetual theme in our discussions about the V-Twin Girls and its promotional arm JM Promotions (named for "Jack and Melissa"). If I resisted an idea, decision or expenditure, I was labeled as unmotivated, unsupportive, and a host of other adjectives. If I resisted insults that masqueraded as criticism, I was hyper-sensitive and "couldn't handle" the reality of business. And since his vision constituted *the* vision, any resistance I offered to his business concepts was labeled a lack of dedication to our marriage.

As Jack transformed the website from a hobby into a business, he entrenched me in figurehead positions of V-Twin Girl team leader and CEO of JM Promotions. Although these titles were ostensibly for my benefit, later events proved that Jack created them to evade responsibility and render me a scapegoat for his poor business choices. It's impossible for me to count the decisions or expenditures he made without my knowledge, thereby placing me in an awkward position with clients or team members. His impulsive spending further undermined my ability to pay the girls for appearances, especially when he'd just announced, "Oh, by the way, I just bought concert tickets for the receptionist at the Harley dealership." When Jack referred the girls' inquiries to me, I was cast as the incompetent CEO. My roles were as varied as Jack's lies: a pregnant stripper, a lazy wife who shunned domestic chores, and an incompetent businesswoman.

As Jack persistently attempted to craft a performance team with our group, an extra role was added to my repertoire: arrhythmic dancer. Although Jack lauded my early performances, his critique intensified as he described me as wooden and inflexible. I explained that additional stress created by his behavior didn't create an environment conducive to free-flowing movement, but my reminder fell on deaf ears. "That's just an excuse!" he often said.

"It's weird, though. Earlier in our marriage you claimed I was a good dancer. What changed your mind?"

Without answering my question, Jack trivialized my skill by invoking my former profession. "You're good at the sensual strip dancing, but when it comes to choreographed moves, you suck."

"You know what the trouble with you is?" he continued as we left a dance practice. "You're just stiff. You're one of those types that needs a few drinks to loosen up before a performance."

"I don't need drinks; I just need less stress," I replied.

"But that's it, Melissa! That's what it is, I swear."

If anything truly made Jack swear, my arrhythmia was not the only thing. It ranked somewhere below financial stress and Linda's lawsuit. In the last days of January, I accompanied him to his first court date in her civil proceeding. Although she wasn't present, her attorney was. After the two emerged from the conference room, Jack said, "Okay, that's it. I walked in and told the magistrate I was filing bankruptcy. Linda's attorney nodded, closed his briefcase, and all of us left the room."

"That's pretty standard procedure," I explained.

We returned home, where I retired to the basement for my usual workout. I emerged from the basement a sweaty mess. As I walked to the kitchen sink to grab a glass of water, I saw Jack reading a monthly magazine entitled *Anabolic Insider*. When I inquired, he freely admitted he'd tried a few performance enhancing substances in the past but no longer indulged.

"Ever since I bought that stuff, they keep sending me these newsletters," he said, tossing the publication on the counter. I began leafing through it, pausing at a photo of a curvy woman dubbed as the "Anabolic Insider Babe" for April. Jack shivered. "She's too muscular for me."

"Maybe so," I said, "but she's got some good definition."

"Have you ever tried any of that stuff before? The steroids, I mean."

"Never any steroids, but one fat burner supplement," I replied, as I described how I stopped immediately after my first dosage made me feel like I was going to have a heart attack. "I hopped off the treadmill and never took another one again."

"Did you ever try anything else?" he asked.

"No, but I was always curious about something I saw advertised in a GNC circular. It started with a t, I think it was called Taraxatone. It looked like it was designed to enhance muscular definition, rather than build energy."

"Maybe you should consider trying it for the photo shoots and appearances. Couldn't hurt."

"I dunno about that," I replied. "The product's probably a glorified diuretic, and with my history of urinary infections, it might be pretty dangerous."

"It might not be hazardous if you don't take the full amount," he said. "Maybe just a moderate dosage."

"I'd rather not," I said. What ensued was another speech about my lack of dedication to the website. I wasn't "devoted to the mission," he claimed, an oft-repeated military theme that remained unmatched, save for directional references such as "starboard" and "port." In an ill-fated attempt to please Jack, I gave in and purchased my first bottle of the herbal diuretic that was famous among bodybuilders. Although I refused to take it more than five days at a time, it became a regular part of preparation for photo shoots and appearances. It wasn't uncommon for Jack to welcome me home with a kiss and a reminder: "Did ya start taking your stuff?"

In addition to asking me to drink and take supplements, Jack asked me to formulate an agreement that he could take to venues prior to appearances. I made up a standard agreement requiring business operators to pay us a nominal fee, all of which would be divided up among the team members. My share, of course, was funneled back to recoup expenses, a fact I freely accepted during our group's infancy.

As our appearances grew in early 2005, Jack presented the agreement to venues across Northeast Ohio. There was an exception, one which led to the single highest financial loss Jack and I sustained during the V-Twin Girls' existence. Ironically, the event wasn't remembered among our group for our monetary loss, or Jack's oversight regarding the agreement. Rather, its primary claim to fame arose from a fate that befell me at the event itself.

Jack was excited when he began talking with a promoter from Peabody's Concert Club about hosting a motorcycle-related event at the venue. After Grant Keenan expressed interest in having the V-Twin Girls appear at the biker music rally, we began to prepare dance routines for two music montages. Jack prepared posters and ads. Promotion for the event kicked into high gear as the ladies rehearsed routines for our highest profile appearance to date. During planning stages I asked Jack about the payment he negotiated with Grant. He indicated that the team's payment was going to be based upon the amount of tickets sold for the event, as well as the number of attendees. This arrangement required us to sell tickets to generate an income that permitted us to break even. At that point it didn't occur to me to ask Jack whether he'd provided Grant with our standard venue agreement, for I assumed that my husband followed our agreed-upon procedure.

Jack informed our team that we'd be provided with refreshments and non-alcoholic drinks in Peabody's "green room," which would serve as our area for show preparation. I explained to the women that the club was a concert venue rather than a full bar, so they needed to plan accordingly. "They've got beer and a few limited liquors, which you're free to purchase on your own. But if you want something out of the ordinary... whether it's Snapple or Bacardi Breezers, you'll need to bring it. Just avoid publicizing your choice out of respect for the concert club," I said.

One Friday night in April, I headed home from dance practice filled with anticipation. Within twenty-four hours I was scheduled to take the main stage at Peabody's with five other team members. As I rolled into Walmart to pick up some groceries, I began running through the "to do" list in my head: pack my bag, lay out my clothes, etc. I strolled down the bread aisle and grabbed a loaf of Roman Meal for Jack, who had alerted me we were out. After grabbing some milk for the kids, I went to the liquor area and picked up a bottle of Tequila Rose, my beverage of choice.

When I came in the door, I was surprised to be the target of an explosive outburst.

No sooner had I greeted Jack and Jason in the den did I get pelted with a barrage of questions regarding my whereabouts. "Where the hell were you?!?" he demanded.

Like so many recipients of accusatory abuse, I fell into the trap of answering his queries instead of telling him to knock it off. "I was at dance practice, then stopped at the store," I replied.

"You should've been home over half an hour ago!" he yelled.

"I would've been if I hadn't stopped at Walmart," I replied, growing uneasy that thirteen-year-old Jason was an audience for his father's tirade.

"Walmart, huh? Well, you could've given me a fucking phone call!!!!"

"Oh calm down. I didn't feel it was necessary since I'd already told you I was stopping. Don't fuss at me just 'cause you forgot."

He rose from the sofa and walked into the kitchen, where he began opening and closing the cupboards, aimlessly searching for a snack. As he bustled around, I held up my purchases. "I got some bread, 'cause I know you're out. Some whole milk, so you and the kids have it for the morning. Soy milk, so *I* have something in the morning. And my beverage treat." As I put the bottle of Tequila Rose away in the cupboard, I put the plastic grocery bags away.

"I'm gonna take a shower," I said, still reeling from Jack's verbal assault. "Hey, by the way. How's your shoulder?" I asked, hoping to find some insight into his tantrum.

"It hurts a bit, but I feel alright," he mumbled as he wandered to the computer.

Upstairs I attempted to wash away the evening's

negativity as I pondered the motivations behind Jack's outburst. Shoulder pain? Stress over tomorrow's performance? It was hard to determine the impetus for this latest incident, but one thing was sure. These occasions were growing more frequent, and many had no rhyme or reason.

The following day was a flurry of activity. After Theresa picked up the kids, I performed my health and beauty regimen under Jack's watchful eye. As I completed my makeup application and finished my hair, I looked up to see him standing in the bathroom doorway.

"Turn around. Let me see," he said. "Looks good," he said, scanning my face. "Wait," he paused, pointing to a reddish bump covered in concealer. "What's that?" he asked.

"Probably a blemish or zit," I responded.

"Try to put some more makeup on that or something. It's pretty obvious."

"It's already smothered in concealer and powder," I replied. "Applying more may make it worse."

"Just try to cover it up, please?" he asked. "I have enough to deal with today without our team leader looking like a pimply teenager."

I finished up and took my duffel bag downstairs. After retrieving the remainder of my clothes from our laundry room, I grabbed the bottle of Tequila Rose and placed everything in my bag. Following a last-minute once over of its contents, I zipped it up.

"Ready?" Jack asked as he picked up my bag. "Let's go."

We met our team members and carpooled to a brief appearance at an outdoor festival in the sleepy town of Canal Fulton before beginning our hour-long trek to Cleveland. Once the metropolitan skyline greeted our eyes, Jack mapped our itinerary. "Once we get there, we'll get your bags out and get you guys to the green room. While the girls are relaxing, I'll find Grant."

When Jack opened the club's door, invisible clouds of stale smoke billowed out to greet us. We walked past the ticket collectors that were preparing to open the doors. Giggles and excited voices arose from the club's stairwell as we made our way upstairs to the green room, where we opened our makeup bags. About half an hour later, club staff entered the room bearing tubs of bottled water, soda, and a few complimentary beers for the women. I joined my team mates as I opened my beverage of choice, pouring the opaque pink beverage into a plastic cup. As the distant sounds of live music began, yet another staffer came bearing three large pizza boxes.

We assisted each other with cosmetics and hair. Jack eventually came in with Grant, a young portly gentleman who introduced himself before the two retired into the adjacent office. We sipped and munched as a few of the girls mingled with two of the club's male staff, whom Jack had requested remain with us during his discussion with Grant. Despite the fact I rarely ate pizza, I was wary of the dangers of drinking alcohol on an empty stomach. Common sense prevailed over my finicky food habits, so I plucked a slice out of the box. My nose wrinkled in disgust as I pulled cheese strands away from my piece.

"You guys are probably going to go on after this band's second set," one of the fellows announced.

Moments later Grant emerged from the office with Jack, whose face was dark with apprehension. After Grant summoned his staff downstairs, Jack pulled me aside. I walked over, my cup in hand.

"I talked with Grant. Doesn't look like we're gonna get as much money as I thought."

"What d'ya mean?" I asked. "We were supposed to get money from the tickets and the door, right?"

"Yeah," he hesitated, "but ticket sales weren't great. If you look downstairs you can see there's not a big crowd. Looks like we're going to get only about a hundred fifty."

"Didn't you tell me he gave us a minimum guarantee?"

"Yeah," Jack said, shaking his head. "But he says he can't pay up with the ticket sales being so low. There's no money available."

"Did you have him sign that agreement I drew up?"

"He promised he'd pay," Jack insisted.

"That's a no, I suppose. We're gonna have to pay these girls ourselves? Jesus Christ! We don't have the money to do that," I said.

"I know, I know. But we *have* to!"

I heaved a big sigh as I returned to the table and sank into my chair, musing upon the stage performance and monetary hole that awaited me. I attempted to distract myself by assisting other girls and engaging in idle chit chat, but my mind couldn't help but wander to the mortgage that loomed. Just when it seemed Jack and I had caught up, we were pulled back into the morass by his self-destructive pattern. Tears of frustration stung my eyes as I rummaged through my duffel in search of a hair pick. For several months I'd endured the denigration of my education as "useless," a phenomenon that never ceased for the duration of our marriage. Yet the futility of my academic knowledge was created by Jack's utter disregard for my legal advice. I couldn't win.

I returned to my seat and fluffed my curls. As I plunged the styling pick through my tresses, I sensed a vague disorientation coming over me. It wasn't the warmth of an alcohol buzz, a phenomenon I'd already begun to experience an hour ago. It also wasn't the confusion associated with being drunk. Rather, it was an odd numbness I couldn't shake. My hand couldn't feel the same plastic hair instrument I'd just grabbed moments before, nor could I feel one of the girls take it from my grasp as I permitted her to use it. I threw away the remaining third of the strawberry flavored liquor I'd brought with me, fearful that it could worsen my state. In doing so, I nearly tripped over my bag. Although I wasn't sufficiently cognizant to realize my difficulties weren't symptomatic of mere alcohol intoxication, I became increasingly aware of a tingling sensation underneath my skin as my conversational responses grew slower. Suddenly Jack's voice pierced the air as he announced our imminent stage call.

"Okay ladies, let's go!" he said, as he grabbed my duffel bag to carry downstairs. "You ready?" he asked me.

"Yeah," I responded. We followed Jack into the hallway to the stairs. I held onto the railing for dear life as I valiantly attempted to navigate the metal stairs. Jack looked back at me.

"You okay?" he frowned.

"Yep," I said, as I muttered about my high-heeled boots. Anna, one of our team members, reached out her hand.

"Here ya go," she said. "I got ya. My heels aren't as high."

Once we reached stage side, we lined up in formation. The music boomed as we entered the stage for our introductory number. I followed our moves in a slower rhythm that was all too obvious to my team mates. I was ignorant of the snail's pace at which I moved, and I didn't notice my team mate Natasha's hand around my waist as she gently guided me offstage at the song's end. We reached the bottom of the stage steps. The onslaught began.

"What's wrong?" Jack demanded. "It looked like

you were off doing your own thing up there." I reached backward and sank onto the ledge. "What's going on with you?" he said, glaring at me with his usual impatience. I stared blankly ahead. He walked away to speak with a stage hand, but he returned within seconds, pausing in front of me.

"Are you awake?!" he yelled. "Oh my god," he said, his voice sinking as he stared at my face. "You are fucked up! Have you been drinking?"

"Well, yeah," I said meekly, "but it's nothing I haven't had before."

"What was it?" he asked.

"Tequila Rose," I responded. "My usual."

"Where in the hell did you get Tequila Rose?"

"I bought it last night. Don't you remember?" I asked, as I slowly reached for the costume top I was slated to wear on the next musical set.

"No," he said as he grabbed the clothing out of my hand. "No, I don't remember. You kept it from me," he declared as our team members milled about. "There's no way you can go onstage like this." He turned to say something to one of the other girls, then returned his attention to me.

"I'm disappointed in you, ya know? Of all the girls, I never expected this out of you," he said, shaking his finger in my face. He turned to Jacinda, one of our team members who bore a striking resemblance to actress Natalie Portman. I heard muffled chatter and looked up to see Jacinda shaking her head.

"I don't know if she's drunk or if it's something else," Jack said to her. The two looked at me as Jacinda expressed doubt about alcohol.

"I don't think that's it," she said as she drew closer to me. "Look at her eyes. Maybe someone slipped her something."

Jack neared my face. "Maybe you're right. Did

you take anything?" he asked.

"No!" I said. "The only things I've drank here are bottled water and the Tequila Rose." I ran my hand through my hair in abject frustration. I barely had enough sensation in my hand to feel the curls.

"How much was left in the bottle?" Jack asked.

"About a third," I replied. "I've had more than that before."

"Where did you have it?"

"I kept it in my bag most of the time, except when I poured."

"Did you throw it away?"

"Yeah." I wasn't coherent enough to ask why the whereabouts of the bottle mattered, when it was the plastic cup that remained on the table's surface, accessible to passersby inside the green room (an area I never left). Any attempt to spike the *bottle* on the premises would've required rummaging through my bag, an act that would've drawn my immediate attention.

"So much for having that tested! It's probably buried by now." Jack threw up his hands in futility. If only I'd possessed the presence of mind to say, "No! The bottle's black, distinctive, and still in the trash can by the table. Somebody's gotta find it. It'll still be there when our stage show's done. Somebody help. Please!" I lacked the cognizance to issue the demand.

"Oh brother," he said, shaking his head. Even as he appeared to ponder the plausibility that I was drugged, he moved his face inches from mine and said, "I expected better out of you. You can't handle stuff like this. *You're not Natasha!*" It was a veiled reference to our team member's history of substance abuse.

"I'm sorry," I said. "I only wanted to loosen up like you wanted me to."

"Don't blame me. I never told you to do *this*!" he exclaimed as he walked over to grab the same camera he'd childishly demanded weeks prior to Christmas. He zoomed in for a close-up. My eyes blinked at the flash, a sign that not all my sensory perception was annihilated. In an act meant to punish me, Jack later displayed this snapshot of my face several times on our home computer screen with continual rebukes.

Moments later, Natasha approached me and scanned my face. She glanced furtively at Jack. Once his face was turned, she whispered, "Did you take anything?"

"No. I only had that Tequila Rose, I swear! And I've had it before."

"Honey, your pupils are really small," she said, laying a hand on my shoulder. "You think someone slipped you something?" Powerless to offer an explanation, I put my head in my hands and began to cry. Natasha put her arm around me.

In seconds I became aware that Jack and Anna were talking several feet away. Jack dipped a plastic cup into the nearby cooler and splashed cold water onto my back. "Oh my God," Anna said. It took several minutes for me to notice the wetness. I reached around and clumsily wiped my back, when I heard her voice again. "That's not liquor."

Despite the fact that everyone seemed painfully aware I was drugged, it didn't stop the tongue-lashing Jack dished out. For a husband who expressed fear that he "might need to" take me to a hospital, his energy was focused on the show- not just the stage show, but the one created by his tirade. Just as Howard K. Stern ignored a stumbling Anna Nicole's need for medical attention, Jack displayed a similar "The show must go on" mentality. It seemed more important to berate me in front of the team, rather than spirit me to an emergency room while the girls performed in our absence. His tirade even concerned the girls, one of whom approached him privately to ask a bold-faced question that angered him. "You're not going to beat her, are you?" After returning to the green room for a final check for forgotten items, Jack returned downstairs. He continued to vent as we pulled out of the parking lot.

"They think I'm gonna beat you!" he protested. "I told the girls to meet at our house tomorrow at noon and we'll pay them. You'll have to give them checks." To lose over six hundred dollars at a time we could least afford it was the final insult to a traumatic evening. Jack continued to upbraid me, but eventually he gave up the assault. "You're probably not hearing me anyway."

I awoke in the morning to a watered-down version of the previous evening's tirade. "We're going to make a new rule. No team member can drink before a performance! I couldn't tell what it was... your pupils weren't dilated. They were more constricted than anything else. Could've been a combination of things: a rufie, alcohol, who knows. But you opened yourself up for it! I didn't know if I was gonna have to take you to the hospital. You let me down. You let the girls down. You're gonna apologize to them when they come over."

As the girls filed in our doorway, each hugged me and asked whether I was okay. I assured them I was physically fine and had no hangover or withdrawal symptoms. I donned the obligatory sackcloth and ashes as I pulled out our checkbook and paid our team members. Speculation about the evening's events ran rampant through our discussion as the women responded to Jack's inquiries. We collectively denied that anyone other than the three club staff members (including Grant) entered the green room. The gentlemen chatted with a couple of the girls who sat on the side of the table opposite my chair. This fact led to Jack's later speculation that Grant himself spiked my drink in a concerted effort to get access to Selina, his favorite V-

Twin Girl. ("What better way to get to Selina, by getting me and you out of the club?") He repeated this speculation to several, including his son Jack Jr., to whom he reported that he was "pretty sure" he knew who drugged me, but "couldn't prove it."

The coming weeks saw repeated references to the incident as Jack vacillated between blaming my alleged drunkenness and an unknown drug for my condition. Like a persistent weed, the issue resurfaced in a 2006 conversation we had in our computer room. After saying, "Grant called the other day," he gas lighted me, claiming that the promoter told him that he'd observed me snorting cocaine with Natasha that fateful evening. Captured in his conversational web, I issued my defensive denial and pointed out, "But Grant knows I'm your wife and an attorney. Pretty stupid of him to make that allegation. I think I'll e-mail him." Jack urged me to let the matter drop, saying, "Ah he's probably just trying to redirect attention away from himself."

It was impossible for me to determine the true chain of events that led to my condition that evening. Without the benefit of an emergency room visit, I couldn't identify the nefarious substance. However, the extensive quest for drug information I later conducted helped me to discern that many of my symptoms were not normal indications of rohypnol (a/k/a "rufie") or alcohol ingestion. This was especially true of my phenomenon widely known by physicians as "pinpoint pupils." Instead of the standard rufie, the likely culprit was an opiate-based narcotic, whether it was a street drug like heroin or a prescription such as Oxycontin or Percocet.

Regardless of the mysterious circumstances surrounding that night, it was an especially telling event in our marriage and the fledgling website. Not only did it reveal Jack's tendencies to our team ("You're not going to beat her, are you?"), but it provided yet another example of his financial recklessness and disregard for my physical well-being. I felt helpless as these proclivities worsened, resigning myself to a fate that seemed all but inevitable.

8. LOSING LIFE

I lost everything today.
I got so beaten I ran away.
I lost everything today.
I can't find my way to yesterday.
- Ra, "I Lost Everything Today"

Weeks following the fiasco at Peabody's Concert Club, I celebrated my thirty-fifth birthday. Perhaps "celebrated" is an over-exuberant word. "Observed" is better. During my marriage, I learned to observe special occasions instead of celebrate them. It was a contrast to the approach taken by my family, who always found a way to commemorate these days regardless of economic circumstance. Two dollars and fifty cents bought the cake mix and icing, but effort and love purchased a true celebration. I turned thirty-five with little fanfare, save for a card that Jack handed me before reminding me that I had to pick up Natasha for the evening's dance practice.

"You're kidding, aren't you?" I asked. "She and I are the only ones available. The other girls are working or in class, so it's a wash with just us. Besides it's my birthday. We may not have much money right now, but the very least we can do is spend it together."

"The two of you can still get a lot accomplished. Natasha's a better dancer than you, and you need work," he said. "We gotta stay ready in case someplace calls us for an appearance. Duty falls on birthdays too, but that's part of the mission. Maybe this weekend I'll cook your favorite: pecan-crusted chicken salad."

At that point I had two options, neither of which had palatable consequences. I could rebel by cancelling the practice in observation of my own birthday, thereby forcing me to observe the occasion at home in stony silence with Jack. Or I could pick Natasha up as planned, with the minimal benefit of spending a few of my birthday hours with a "sister" of sorts whose compassion towards me was readily apparent the night I was drugged. I chose the latter. In the meantime I secretly looked forward to Mother's Day weekend, when Jack and I were slated to meet my parents for dinner in a dual celebration of both occasions.

I turned thirty-five amidst financial loss that permeated the entire year. Questionable tactics employed by Jack's mortgage company led to the dismissal of his bankruptcy, the end result of which was the resumption of Linda's lawsuit and reappearance of debts from his past. Like Benazir and Anna Nicole, I was continually saddled with the dubious financial legacy and monetary misdeeds of the man I loved. Just like Howard K. Stern and Asif Ali, Jack engaged in a pattern of financially selfish decisions that brought down many women in his life, including me. His secretive promissory note to Linda was the tip of the iceberg. Demands for items beyond our budget, disregard of the business contracts I drew up, and exploitation of my assets were all examples of irresponsibility that detrimentally affected me. Like Anna, the sexually charged public image I assumed made it easy for Jack to claim I was a willing beneficiary of his promotional skill. Yet few knew the price I paid for his so-called skill, both figuratively *and* literally.

The price I paid didn't go unnoticed by the furry members of our household, especially my grey kitty Artemis, whose name ironically arose from the Greek goddess that protected women. The feeling was mutual, for Jack had developed a distaste for the feline with two habits that grated on his narcissistic nerves. Not only did her penchant for urinating on his clothing annoy him, but he abhorred the fact she fought his rough flea grooming.

As Artie's battle with Jack waged on, the summer

became an ill-fated season for another feline member of our household. One morning at about 9:30 I received a phone call at my office. At the other end of the line was a panic-stricken Jack who announced something was seriously wrong with Poof, the spunky stray he'd adopted several months ago. I asked what was wrong.

"I don't know," he said, his voice shaking. "After I put Jill on the bus this morning, I didn't see him around. Something told me to open up the basement door. When I did, he was laying at the bottom of the stairs. I picked him up and set him on his feet, but he couldn't walk. I think one of his legs is broken or something." I winced at the thought of Jack trying to make a lame cat walk. My mind raced and I asked the million dollar question.

"What happened?" I looked at my clock; it had been an hour and a half since Jill was put on the bus. I wondered how long the cat had been injured.

"I don't know," he repeated tearfully. "It's one of his legs, that's for sure. Maybe one of the weights downstairs fell over on him. I didn't know what to do. I took him upstairs and laid him on our bed for awhile. He messed up our bedspread; I had to put it in the washer."

"What d'ya mean?" The knot in my stomach grew larger as Jack talked.

"He pooped on our bed while he lay there," he explained. I didn't think to ask why he wasted valuable time washing our bedspread when our pet needed urgent care.

"Then either he's so bad off that his bowels are giving out, or he's really nervous," I said. The only time I recalled Poof pooping on a forbidden surface was an occasion when Jack combed him for fleas in his classically gentle manner.

"I gotta take him to an emergency vet or something!"

"Obviously," I said. "I don't know where we'll find

the money. I had to use an emergency vet once and it cost seven hundred dollars."

"I'll sell one of my guns or something," he said. "I don't care. I just gotta get him somewhere. I might take him to that clinic in Navarre, down the road."

"Okay. Let me know what they say." A broken shoulder was the culprit. At least that's the diagnosis Jack reportedly received from the vet, who graciously permitted us to pay the $800 bill in two installments. After surgery, Poof was sent home with a pin in his shoulder and an awkward limp. The following day, Jack appeared infuriated at an allegation made by Theresa over the phone. "You know what she said to me?" he asked indignantly.

"What?" I asked.

"She asked me why I threw Poof down the stairs!"

"Where would she get something like that?"

"I don't know. She's just a bitch." He walked away to the computer desk, apparently forgetting that he'd already told on himself by revealing a key incident of animal cruelty. On a couple occasions Jack referenced the fact that he'd severely injured the muzzle of Hunter, a family dog he owned during his marriage to Theresa. In discussions with me he passed off the canine's injury as a product of post-traumatic stress disorder, brought about by his military heroics. Could it be possible, I wondered, that Theresa's memory of the incident led her to deduce Jack's cruelty with Poof?

While Poof recuperated from shoulder surgery, Artie's relationship with Jack deteriorated. Her last act of vengeance drew rage that he barely contained. One day my workout was interrupted when Jack opened the basement door.

"Melissa!" he yelled. "You gotta come up here right now!"

I ascended the stairs to find the source of his latest outburst. He raised his hand, revealing a small trickle of blood running down his thumb. He pointed to a large orange bucket that sat beside his feet. "We have to do something about this fucking cat. This is the third time she's bit me. This time she drew blood! It was all I could do not to throw her outside....but I put her in this pail." His finger shook in the bucket's direction. "That's the last time!"

"You need to clean up your hand, hon." I looked inside the oblong ventilation hole in the pail's top and saw two panic stricken eyes staring at me. "We'll think of something," I assured him.

"I know what we need to do," he said, as I heard water running in the bathroom. "She needs to go. Period. What if she ever does this to the kids?" he demanded.

"But she's never done it to the kids. I don't understand. Do you think it's because of how you groom her?" I asked, as I slowly opened up the pail and picked her up.

"Look, I *have* to keep her still. She moves around so damned much. I'm not gonna have her be the only animal with fleas in her fur....and for what? Just 'cause she can't handle being groomed?" he said. He emerged from the bathroom, enraged that I was petting Artie.

"Oh great! She bites me and you go and pet her. Thanks for rewarding her!" He threw the towel on the counter top in disgust.

"I'm trying to calm her down," I replied. "For whatever reason, she's upset. Animals just don't do that for the hell of it. Something's seriously wrong." Despite my attempts to reason with Jack, I sensed that Artie's days at our house were numbered.

"I tell you what's wrong. She's a psycho cat that

has no place here. If it was Minnie or Sammie that bit you, I'd get rid of them in a heartbeat!"

"Okay, I'll start calling around to see if a local shelter has space for her." Eventually I forced myself to agree with the logic that Artie's erratic behavior posed a threat to the household. Upon learning that Stark County animal shelters were full, I decided to take her to the Lorain County Animal Protective League. The following week, I left early for work one morning and loaded Artie into my car. I said goodbye to the faithful grey companion whose only crime was to rebel against the person who tormented her and verbally abused her human 'mom." I left the facility's parking lot with a sadness I couldn't shake.

Weeks following Artie's departure, the time arrived for Jack to return to court in Linda's lawsuit. His tension increased as he demanded legal advice from me. Like a broken record, I reiterated that the law wasn't in his favor, so he'd better set his sights on working out a compromise. At July's end, their mediation conference produced a settlement requiring him to grant Linda an interest in the property and remit monthly payments to her.

As our financial woes and marital dysfunction increased, my body reacted to the stress in the only manner it knew. It developed infections in the most private regions imaginable: my urinary and reproductive organs. Not surprisingly they correspond with the sacral chakra, an area that New Age philosophers associate with base emotion, sexuality, and relationships. As my most intimate relationship grew increasingly destructive, urinary tract and yeast infections plagued me on a regular basis. While Jack's reaction to my distress vacillated between blaming my hygiene and the torrid sexual history he imagined, his most common response was one of sexual frustration: "Oh great, I guess this means we can't have sex for awhile!" I, however, was grateful to have a reprieve from the activity that had begun to feel like a duty rather than a passionate expression. One thing was sure, however: I could not turn to my husband for empathy. I learned this during the summer of 2005, when I suffered my first UTI during our marriage.

As we returned one warm evening after a V-Twin Girl meeting at the Hog Heaven, I conveyed my suspicion to him. "You remember me talking about those symptoms I was noticing yesterday?" I asked. "It's definitely a urinary infection. I think it would be best if we head to an ER while we're out. That way I can get a urinalysis, antibiotic, and I'll be on my way without missing any time from work tomorrow."

"What?! You're kidding me?" he roared in a rage that stunned me. "You think you need to go to a hospital for *that*? It's not life-threatening!"

"It's not right now, but it can be if you wait. But why wait, especially when I've got health insurance that will cover the visit? If I start the medication tonight, I'll feel decent enough to go to work tomorrow."

"I've dated girls who've had that before. You should be able to drink cranberry juice and feel fine."

"Well, I actually *have* had it before, Jack. I'm a veteran of these things. Cranberry juice doesn't cure an infection that already exists. Antibiotics are necessary."

"Oh brother," he said, rolling his eyes as we approached our driveway. "It's a good thing you aren't in the military."

Had I known then what I do today, I would've retorted, "It ain't like you were dodging bullets, Mr. Navy SEAL wannabe. Get your wife to a hospital, you self-righteous bastard." Instead I succumbed to a passivity that was alien to me, one which didn't even allow me to drive myself to the hospital. That move would've forced me to admit that I had to rely on myself and not my husband to look out for my physical health, something I wasn't ready to do. It was easier on my psyche to think, "*Maybe it's not so bad. I'll just wait and go to a clinic during my lunch hour tomorrow.*" I remained at home, peeing blood and twisting and turning for a comfortable seating position on the sofa. After a sleepless night, I drove to work and asked one of the clerks, "Where's the nearest outpatient clinic around here?"

After I explained my problem, my supervisor at the intake department had no difficulty letting me take an extra hour on my lunch. She encouraged me to go home after I returned from the clinic. My fellow magistrate Joanne said, "I don't even know why you're here anyway …you can't even sit well in your chair. Sheesh!" I longed to explain why home was the last place I wanted to be, but my desire to go to bed was stronger. I called Jack at work to tell him I was coming home early. Once I put my key in our door, I went upstairs for a much-needed nap.

Several hours later, I stirred when Jack walked in the bedroom and asked how I was feeling. "You getting up for dinner?"

"I think so," I replied.

"So how long do you have to take that stuff?"

"If I remember right, I've gotta take the antibiotic for ten days."

"Does that mean you can't have sex for ten days?" he asked.

"Actually, I was told to avoid sexual activity for two weeks."

"That sucks," he said.

Mere days after full recuperation from my UTI, Jack came upstairs one night with an odd observation.

"You're pretty popular today, almost too much. The numbers on your photo page tripled in the last twenty-four hours."

"Did you promote my pictures on any other

website, or add any links?" I asked. Jack shook his head.

"No. You don't think the people where you work have seen the website, do you?"

"I don't know," I shrugged. "I suppose it's possible. But hey, there's no topless or obscene shots of me on there... so even if someone at court saw the site, the most they can do is gossip."

"You think so?" he asked.

"Well there's nothing I'm doing that violates my employee handbook. It's my off-duty personal hobby and none of their business." Those were my famous last words.

The following day Jolene, my supervisor at the intake department, approached me and said, "I got a call from downtown today. Dale Lugar, the assistant administrator, wants to meet with you and me today at the Justice Center at 3:00."

"Really? Did he say what it was about?" I asked as my brow furrowed and gut churned.

"No," she said. "It was funny. I asked him, and he said he preferred not to go into it on the phone. I figure you and I can leave here around 2:45; that should give us enough time."

I knew before we walked into the office. Jolene and I sat on opposite sides of the twenty-something lad whose managerial star had steadily rose in the court's elite. He took a deep breath as he explained that he'd called us downtown to discuss a matter that had been brought to his attention, one which had caused consternation among several at the juvenile court. Then came the $20,000 question: "Are you familiar with a group called the V-Twin Girls?"

"Yes, I am," I said honestly. I proceeded to describe our team and my off-duty hobby.

"So you are the person identified as "Kitten' on

the website?"

"Yes," I replied. "It's our custom to use nicknames to maintain security of team members."

"Do you and your husband generate income from the website?" Dale inquired, attempting to ferret out whether he could label my hobby a "part-time job" requiring me to notify the court.

"Although my husband and I have discussed that possibility, we have no immediate plans in that direction. It's currently a hobby that allows us to perform outreach in the biker communities, and that's how it will stay for the time being."

"Have you ever shared this hobby with anyone at work?"

"I haven't volunteered it in discussions, but I haven't taken excessive effort to keep it a secret either. After all, the website is listed in several internet search engines and our events are open to the public."

"Well," Dale sighed, "I appreciate you coming down here and answering these questions. I'm sure you can understand why some concern was raised about the site. I want to make it clear this is merely an investigatory meeting, there's no decision that's been made regarding the sit. I just wanted to find out a little more about it, that's all. If I receive any additional information or reach any conclusions, I'll contact both of you."

"Thank you," I said. "Please feel free to let any 'concerned' party know that they're more than welcome to attend one of our events or charity benefits if they'd like to see us for themselves. As a matter of fact, it might alleviate their concern."

"Okay, I appreciate it," he said flatly as he shook my hand.

The atmosphere at home was rife with gloom and doom as Jack railed against the legal system in a "woe is me" speech. I understood his frustration, but I needed a partner to assist me with strategy. That was impossible when he was in the middle of a self-serving speech about what "we" would lose if and when the court fired me.

"Yes, the system sucks. I could sit for hours and whine about how our culture doesn't want a woman to be smart and sexy, but I don't have time to dispense commentary. This is our time to plan what to do if the court falls prey to the cultural double standard. I need to know if you'll help me fight it."

"You're my wife," he said. "Of course I'll help you fight it. I'll go down and pop their heads off, one by one. Five or six more doesn't make a difference to me. Face it, Melissa. They're gonna screw you."

It was a sentiment echoed by my magistrate colleague Joanne, who warned me to take an attorney when Dale summoned me back downtown. "I'm telling you, girl. You better take somebody. Look at what they did to Tonnie, the girl who worked down the hill at the shelter."

"You're probably right," I said. "But if that's what they intend to do, they'll just be handing my notice to me anyway. The time I'll need to have an attorney will be at the hearing."

"Start looking around now, Melissa. You need someone who doesn't mind challenging the system and the judges, and not every attorney in Lorain County will do that."

"Yeah, I will."

"Man, I'm telling you what," Joanne said shaking her head. "If they want to start following employees around to see what they're doing during their off time, they might wanna start with the probation department. Makes me sick. They've got a lot of nerve to let a two-time DUI offender who's been sued for sexual harassment head up probation, and here you're the spawn of Satan because you appear on-line in a bikini!

Gimme a break!"

"Sexual harassment? What? Did I miss something?" I asked.

"Yes, sexual harassment! It was years ago, before you got here. Nellie Mulligan was sued for sexual harassment, had problems for her off-duty partying. And you know what? She's still here. They better not give you a speech about the court's image when they got her ass in such a high position. And we won't even talk about the employees that hang out in strip clubs."

"But that's it," I protested. "I didn't even *break the law* or endanger others! I appeared on-line in the same thing I could legally wear to a beach. And they hand me this self-righteous crap! Like, 'Oh, we've gotta investigate' as if their employee's been busted for armed robbery."

"That's what I'm saying Melissa. These are the hypocrites you're dealing with, and they're the ones in charge. Again, you *need* to find an attorney to take with you if this goes to a hearing. And I think it will."

She was right. Several days later, following my morning child support hearings, I received a call from an administrative secretary downtown. I was to come the following day to the justice center for a meeting with Mr. Lugar and Bob Canter, the court's chief of probation and youth services (i.e., my supervisor's boss). I asked the secretary point blank if this "meeting" was an employment hearing, and she indicated it was merely a meeting at which Mr. Lugar intended to convey some "pertinent information." The information conveyed to me was that I was suspended for two weeks with pay, pending the outcome of a hearing that would determine my fate with the juvenile court. Dale handed me a piece of paper with this "pertinent information," and asked me if I had any questions or items to add. After reading from the paper that my suspension was due to a purported failure to report part-time employment, I replied, "Yes, I do."

"Although I recognize the decision that's been made, I neither support nor agree with the reasoning. I disagree with your characterization of the website as 'employment,' and it's my belief that a deeper reason underlies my suspension."

"I understand what you're saying," he nodded with pseudo-empathic listening, "and you'll have every opportunity to voice those concerns at the hearing. You'll be able to call witnesses and have counsel available, if you choose. Do you have any other questions?"

"Not at this time," I said succinctly.

As we rose, Bob Canter walked me outside as we engaged in a philosophical conversation about our culture and the legal system. A kindly gentleman in his early fifties, he was a court veteran who'd seen, and undoubtedly felt, the sting of the judgmental establishment for which he worked. He explained that he never knew about the V-Twin Girls until Judge Pamela Levy (one of the court's three judges) opened the link and raised a stink with the court administration. "I gotta hand it to you, Melissa. I admire the way you conducted yourself in there. I also respect you for being unapologetic about your pursuits."

"Well, Bob," I said, "I didn't see how a tantrum would solve anything. Despite what some people perceive, I *am* a professional with dignity." I smiled wryly.

"Yes, I see that in you. By the same token," he said thoughtfully as he cocked his head, "can you also see how the judges might react negatively to those images?"

"You know," I said thoughtfully, "I can see how the photos might raise eyebrows for some with issues about women and sexuality, but raised eyebrows don't give them carte blanche to affect someone's livelihood. I was taught that a court isn't supposed to cloud its reasoning with cultural bias. This," I said, motioning upward at the brick building, "is supposed to be the place where people come to avoid bias, not walk right into it."

"Good point," he nodded. "But those judges are people. I remember when people raised a lot of eyebrows over Judge Levy's divorce, and employees were looking at the on-line court records in her case. She forced the court to keep them private."

"Interesting," I said. "That's normally a public record."

"I guess she felt she had to protect her privacy," he said as we walked down the steps. "She oversees divorces and sentences juveniles on dangerous felonies."

"Yeah, but if a dangerous juvenile wanted to track her down, he could do it whether or not her divorce is out there. Plus, her kids are all adults. Maybe there's other issues she didn't want raising the eyebrows of employees. I suppose that's her decision. But her marital problems don't lessen her authority anymore than the website lessens mine. If we lock a kid up, the result is the same whether she's divorced or if I sit on a Harley in a bikini at the day's end....ya know?"

"True," he laughed.

"Oh well. You know, I'd have more respect if they admitted it's the raised eyebrows, and not this 'un-reported job' excuse. I'll see if they fess up, I guess."

"Good luck Melissa." He shook my hand. "I hope things go well for you," he said warmly. Although I intuited his sincerity, I didn't fathom its depth. Weeks following our discussion on the courthouse steps, he resisted a demand from the administration that he write a letter decrying my purported lack of professionalism. I didn't learn of his gesture for several months. Nevertheless, his refusal to participate in the court's political game earned my undying respect.

I drove back to the intake department, where my

colleague Joanne nodded. "Hate to say I told you so, but...What reason are they giving you?"

"That I didn't report 'part-time employment' per the court's policy. That's their approach; they're claiming the website is a for-profit business and I'm employed by it."

"Well, I was talking with Carlita...ya know, Judge Berris' magistrate downtown. She agreed that you're gonna need an attorney who's not afraid. The first words out of her mouth were 'Jeremy Rosenblatt.'"

"Rosenblatt, the old prosecutor?" I asked.

"Yeah, you know, the one who was let go by the county prosecutor 'cause he didn't play along with a plea bargain for that high-ranking official in Avon, oh....what's his name," she tapped her forehead, "I can't remember. But anyway, he's been burned for not playing politics. He's got no problem ruffling a judge's feathers. And the best thing?"

"What's that?" I asked.

"He hates Judge Levy. Their bad blood goes way back. I think she owes him money for helping with her divorce."

"Really? He helped with the same divorce where the records are private?"

"Yup. I bet he'd love an opportunity to challenge her."

"Wow," I replied. "I've never met Rosenblatt himself, but defense attorneys used to bitch about him all the time. They said he was nasty."

"Of course they did, 'cause he didn't play the backroom deals and plea bargains that keep the system going. He doesn't roll like that. He'd be a good one to take with you."

"Alright," I said. "I'll give him a call tomorrow." I rose and walked out to the parking lot.

Meanwhile, the reception I received at home was

less than uplifting. Any hope I'd had of hearing "I'm sorry honey; I know how much that job means to you" was dashed as soon as I walked in the door.

"Well?" he asked, leaning against the kitchen counter. "What did they say?" I handed him the paper.

"See for yourself," I said.

"Just tell me!" he said, tossing the letter aside. "Are you fired?"

"Not technically, but I think that's where they're headed. I'm suspended with pay until the hearing in a couple weeks. There's an attorney I'm gonna call tomorrow and make an appointment with him. He's one of the only Lorain County lawyers that has the stomach to challenge a court system."

"Please!" he waved his hand dismissively. "He's a lawyer. Lawyers can't do shit. Great! What are we gonna do?"

"We're gonna fight, presumably." I said. "You're still with me, right?"

"Of course, but they're gonna do whatever they want," he said, as he turned and wandered to the computer desk. "I tell ya, Melissa," he said, pointing to one of my posters on the computer screen. "This might as well be a business for us. That stupid court system of yours might force us to make it one!"

"We may eventually turn it into one," I said, "but it's never going to be my primary job."

"Why the fuck not?" he demanded. "Your looks and body get you more than that law degree anyway."

"I earned this degree, and the state says I can practice law. Until they say I can't, justice is my occupation...in one form or another. Sure I earned money from my looks in the dancing days, but it was for a short time, so I could continue to my real goal."

"And I bet you made more doing that than you did practicing law. Am I right?"

"On an hourly basis, yes, but money wasn't my ultimate goal. It still isn't, but that doesn't mean I'm not going to fight for my paycheck. We have bills to pay, and this website is *far* from being able to pay our bills. We lose money on it, actually."

"But that won't be forever. If we put the time into it, we can make it solvent."

"True," I said. "But it requires us to tide ourselves over with other income. You've got the radio station, which basically pays your child support and a few utilities. I want to stay at the court until I decide to leave... not when some small-minded bureaucrat tells me to."

"I believe you," he said. "But this is where it's at," he said pointing again to the computer screen. As he regressed into a rant about the futility of lawyers and the justice system, I pondered my strategy. First things first: Call Rosenblatt tomorrow, pick up my paycheck Friday. I prayed for Jack's support, but he was too busy turning me into a profit-bearing cash cow to shoulder the burden of my upcoming struggle. I began to strategize plans for the hearing and ponder a witness list, while he plotted V-Twin Girl stardom. While he edited some bike photos for the website, I called Rosenblatt's office and left a message.

Our phone rang the next day. "Hello," I said.

"Jeremy Rosenblatt. You left a message last night regarding an employment matter, correct?"

"That's correct," I said, before giving him a synopsis of my situation. "The matter is time-sensitive, because I have a hearing before the court administrator next week."

"Can you come to my office Wednesday around two thirty?"

"Sure," I said, smiling as he echoed the same advice I used to give plaintiffs in employment cases.

"Bring your suspension letter and your employee

handbook with you. I might want to copy them while you're here."

I walked into the hallway of the building that hosted offices of several attorneys, including Rosenblatt. I opened his door and walked into a dimly lit lobby area. I knocked on the interior door to ensure he was present.

"Come on in," he shouted. It became apparent that he was finishing up a phone conversation, so I busied myself gazing at the military memorabilia lining his wall. He was by all account a U.S. Marine who took pride in his history. Suddenly I heard his door open wider and looked up to see a slender bald gentleman approach me with an outstretched hand.

"Jeremy Rosenblatt," he said with a penetrating gaze. "Sorry about the lighting," he said, as he reached for a few switches. "I just returned from court moments before you walked in. Then the phone rang." He made his way around end tables with the speed of lightning. What he lacked in physical stature, he made up for with the sheer force of his presence.

"Have a seat," he motioned towards the chairs in front of his desk. "So," he plopped down, "tell me about Juvenile Court. What happened?"

I poured out the entire story as he periodically interjected a few brief questions.

"So you and your husband operate this website...what is it, again, v-twin girls?"

"V-twinGirls.com," I replied as he turned to look up the website on his desktop.

"And you go around to bike events and charities. You guys don't make any money off this?"

"No," I said, as I explained that Jack and I had accepted payment a couple of times that helped defray expenses. "We actually lose money from it."

"Then how in the world are they saying this is part-time employment?" He clicked on my photo page.

"'Kitten', huh? This is you?"

"Yes, that's me. All the ladies use nicknames to preserve security on the website, and Kitten's my chosen label. Since we've been doing this, I've been careful to ensure that the photos aren't topless or obscene. There's been one photo shoot that involved thong swimwear, but those pictures weren't used. I can safely say there's nothing on that website I couldn't wear on Erie Beach. Any of the juveniles or their parents could run into me there, too."

"Yeah," he said, "but they're responding to the sexual appeal of the photos. It's not about being 'employment' at all, they just don't want a magistrate posing in a bikini."

"But they don't have the courage to say that. They might try to bring in other provisions of the handbook, like trying to say I was engaging in conduct that reflected negatively on the court, or.... That I engaged in activity that presented a conflict. Something like that."

"Have you ever used your real name on the site?" he asked.

"No."

"'Conflict' relates to financial conflicts of interest, especially when it comes to judges and magistrates. You're not using your real name or position at the court to exert influence on your website, and vice versa. You have no real conflict. You're not engaged in illegal activity, so it's hard for me to imagine that appearing in a bikini reflects negatively on the legal system. Have you been able to determine how this became known?"

I explained what Bob had told me about how the link was sent to Judge Levy, and that she was the only one of the three judges who opened it. "It's not clear who sent her the link, but obviously she took offense. This 'investigation' was initiated and Lugar called me downtown to verify it was me in the photos," I said.

"Pamela Levy had a problem with it. Hah!" He threw back his head, howling with laughter. "When did Levy get all pious? She's the last one who should have a problem with a court employee dressing provocatively. Hell, I remember when I was her supervisor at the prosecutor's office. I had to take her aside and discuss the length of her mini-skirts. Oh boy." He paused for a moment, "If I remember correctly, she's not the administrative judge right now. Of the three, I'm pretty sure it's Devin Beranski. If the hearing's outcome before the administrator isn't favorable, your appeal will be before him."

"What's your opinion of him?"

"When it comes to something like this, it's hard to tell. I think he'd be your best bet among the three judges to hear the appeal. He's a bit more progressive, from what I can tell."

"Yeah, but it seems Levy rules the roost up there."

"Sure they stick together a lot. I'm not saying Beranski is a shoe-in, because the word about your site has already spread and he might feel heat to maintain the status quo. But with a topic like this, no way. I'm afraid the two female judges would crucify you. I'm not trying to be sexist, but women judge other women very harshly."

"Tell me about it," I sighed.

"They've got plenty of clowns working up there. They're selectively enforcing these rules. You may have a First Amendment issue, too, if it comes to that. I think I can help you. At the very least I can represent you during your hearing and appeal, if necessary. Hopefully the problem stops then, but we can take one step at a time. I know you're basically laid off right now, so you're not rolling in dough. How much do you think you can pay me?" he asked as we worked out the details of his compensation. He continued as he took my employee handbook to his Xerox machine. "I know you tried to keep the photos tasteful in your mind, but it doesn't matter. The outcome would be the same if you'd posed topless."

"You think so?"

"Of course! Bottom line, this isn't about whether Judge Levy can see your full breast or not. It's about her thinking you look better in a two-piece than she does."

We began to discuss a proposed witness list for the upcoming hearing. I explained that I wanted to offer testimony from two individuals who'd worked with me in different capacities: my fellow magistrate Joanne and Jeff Carusso, a supervisor at the boys' detention home. These people were willing to verify that my off-duty pursuits didn't affect my professionalism

"Alright," he said. "Tomorrow I'll deliver a letter to the administration entering my appearance as your attorney. I'll attach a summons for them to make those two employees available for the hearing. I'll meet you in the hallway on the fourth floor outside the administration about a half-hour beforehand. Can you drop off a payment by Friday?"

"Sure," I said.

"Okay, that would be appreciated. In the meantime, I'm going to look into a few First Amendment theories so we can be prepared for an appeal. I'll e-mail you anything I find out in the way of case law. Feel free to send me anything you feel is pertinent, too."

"Thank you," I said, shaking his hand as I rose to leave.

My apprehension over the entire drama was lessened by Rosenblatt's willingness to help. His reputation for dogged advocacy preceded him, and I was happy to have him in my corner. Jack didn't share my enthusiasm, a fact that was readily apparent when I got home.

"He's the best option in Lorain County, and I got him!" I smiled.

"Yeah? Does he think you can keep your job?"

"He doesn't believe it's a sure thing, and neither do I. But his representation increases my odds. There's nobody I'd rather have fighting for me."

"So," Jack scoffed, "he's not even sure you can get your job back, but he wants your money."

"He cut me a break on fees," I said, "but nobody works for free. The doctor who analyzes blood tests still needs to be paid for his service regardless of the test's outcome."

"He's a lawyer, and he's not gonna change anything!" Jack declared. "You're going to be fired next week and it will be useless."

"It's highly possible I could be fired, Jack. There's a lot of politics he can't change. You have to look to the future when you choose professionals. If I have to sue them, Rosenblatt's the one I want."

"But he's the one who should prevent that."

"This may arrive as a shock, but it's not his job to guarantee an outcome. You're refusing to validate my choice of attorneys, and I can't change your opinion. But rest assured, he'll do his job. Just do yours and support me. That's all I ask."

"I *do* support you," he heaved a big sigh. "I just don't have a good feeling, that's all. I've feared this could happen someday. It's my fault. I should've never put you in this position."

"We both chose this, Jack. Let's not feel sorry for ourselves; we don't have time at this point." I was annoyed that he was directing our conversation so that he could be reassured of *his* blamelessness. His self-pity stripped my patience raw. I rose from the floor where I sat.

"Just take a lesson from your military days. When your team was under fire, what did you do if one of them got hit? I'm sure you didn't stop and say, 'oh boo hoo it's all my fault'? Your comrades wouldn't be moved by a self-serving 'woe is me' speech. You kept your weapon drawn and planned your next move the best you could. I've come to accept you're more upset about losing the income from juvenile court than you are interested in validating my feelings about the job. But the very least you can do is keep your weapon up and stay focused while Rosenblatt leads the charge. Can you manage that?"

"Don't use the military against me. You think I don't support you?" he turned from the computer screen towards me.

"What I said speaks for itself," I replied. "I need you to be a functional member of my team. Remember *I'm* the one under direct fire here. You face the loss of income, but I face more because I might lose a job that makes me happy. I told you when we dated that social justice is the most important career goal to me. I need you to focus less on making Kitten a 24/7 job than helping me keep something that matters to me."

"I know it matters to you. I hate what's happening!" he protested. "They're a bunch of hypocrites talking trash about the woman I love, and they shouldn't get away with it." It sounded nice, but the empathetic declaration wasn't reflected by his overall response to the crisis. Even as he sputtered periodically about wreaking vengeance upon the decision-makers at court, later events proved that he was all too willing to permit my employer to chew me up and spit me out.

I awoke the morning of the hearing filled with anticipation. I got off the elevator and walked to the benches, where Rosenblatt awaited. "Morning," he nodded. "You ready?"

"As ready as I'll ever be," I replied.

"Okay, look here," he said in a low voice. "The hearing will be transcribed by a court reporter, and everyone who testifies will be sworn in. If the topic arises, I'm going to throw out the notion that you'd be willing to quit doing V-Twin if necessary."

"Really? Do you think it will be necessary?" I said. In the outer corners of my mind, I wondered how Jack would react to that proposal.

"Depends on how bad you wanna stay here. It's my responsibility to help you do that. Since it's not an income-bearing activity, you might consider putting it down if it saves your job. It's our position that it's not the court's business to dictate that decision, but it's something to think about."

"Okay," I nodded. Physical appeal aside, I didn't endure seven years of schooling, three bar exams, and student loans just so a bunch of hypocrites could steal my livelihood. Aside from Rosenblatt and a couple supportive colleagues, I was alone in this struggle and the decision was mine. Forced by the system to choose between my beauty and intellect, I chose to prioritize the latter. Moments later, Joanne appeared, then Jeff Carusso. I thanked them for agreeing to testify.

"No problem, ma'am," Jeff replied.

Lugar emerged from an office and asked us if we were ready. "You can come on back," he said, as he motioned Joanne and Jeff to chairs out in the hall. "It's a small room," he explained. "We'll call you when we're ready for your testimony."

I walked in to find the oblong conference table was crowded to capacity. At the head of the table sat Dustin Medgar, the court administrator and decision-maker for the hearing. To his left sat my supervisor Jolene, followed by Lugar, my "prosecutor." Medgar's left side was graced by the county's legal representative, prosecutor Joe Benning and the court reporter, whose equipment was lodged in between the seats. Then came Rosenblatt's chair, followed by my seat of honor. Rosenblatt pulled out my chair and I sat down facing Medgar himself.

Lugar led the charge by pulling several of my V-Twin Girl photos from a manilla folder. "I'd like to enter these as exhibits, please," he said as Medgar nodded approval. "These photographs were retrieved by the court's technology department from various websites, including V-TwinGirls.com and search engines such as Google," he continued as he affixed numbered stickers to each picture. He laid each one on the table as Rosenblatt questioned him about the chain of events that led to my suspension. Lugar described the day that Judge Levy summoned him and Mr. Medgar into her office to look at an image on her computer screen.

"She indicated that an employee had e-mailed her a link to the V-Twin Girls website, and asked whether the person identified as 'Kitten' was Magistrate Dean." Although he didn't identify the employee, future conversations with various staff indicated that the link was e-mailed to the judges by Kristy Hardnett-Robinson, the head of the court's fiscal department *and* wife of detention home employee Jim Robinson. Lugar continued to explain that although Medgar thought it looked like me, neither of them could verify that fact. Judge Levy instructed the two men to "investigate" the matter and address it at their earliest convenience. The implication of her demand was clear. Lugar then called me downtown to ask about the website, and the rest was history. At this juncture, Rosenblatt called Medgar's objectivity into question, in light of the fact he'd already seen the pictures in the highly-charged atmosphere of Judge Levy's office.

"This can hardly be considered a fair and

impartial hearing," he declared of the kangaroo court proceeding, as he pointed out that the decision to fire me was made that day. "Isn't that correct, Mr. Lugar?" Medgar shifted uncomfortably in his seat, scribbling notes on his memo pad.

Lugar continued to describe the drama that unfolded as news of our website spread through the court like wildfire. "I was contacted by several employees and parents who expressed concern about Ms. Dean's pictures, and her ability to serve as a role model for juveniles." Although the parents were never identified, he named several employees that expressed indignation. From the clerk's office to the fiscal department, the superintendent of the boys' detention facility, and even a judge, it appeared that nearly all of my detractors were women. The few males involved, including Lugar and Medgar, were henchmen doing their bidding. It cemented my belief that despite men's superior economic status, women often inflict the harshest damage on each other in our zeal to assuage our insecurities. I was merely one in thousands of women in history targeted by gossip and criticism from "sisters" who couldn't conceptualize a woman with intellect and sexual appeal as an appropriate role model. For me, however, the cattiness had dire consequences.

The dog and pony show continued as my supervisor Jolene testified that my job performance was above average. As I watched her describe my positive reviews, I was plagued with curiosity about her true feelings regarding the drama unfolding in front of us. Due to the speed of the disciplinary measures, I never got a chance to speak with her privately regarding the website. Any negative feelings she might have had were put aside as she explained that she'd never seen me exhibit any conflicts of interest. After Medgar agreed to stipulate that my job performance wasn't hampered by the website's existence, Rosenblatt and I were permitted to let our two witnesses leave. We excused ourselves briefly into the hallway, where we told Joanne and Jeff they were free to go. "Thanks again," I said to each of them.

"Good luck," said Joanne.

When we re-entered the hearing room, it was my turn. I raised my right hand and swore to tell the truth. Prosecutor Benning and Medgar took turns asking me about the V-Twin Girls, the group's activities, and our charitable appearances. At one point I was questioned about whether I'd given any thought to the judges' opinions *prior* to posing on bikes. I explained that I hadn't because I felt it was not in their purview to dictate my off-duty activities as long as I wasn't breaking the judicial canon of ethics or any applicable laws. Eventually Benning asked whether I intended to continue my activities with the website.

"At this point I intend to continue as long as I'm physically able to do so, yes," I said as I looked up to see a half-smile crossing Medgar's face. Medgar then inquired about my willingness to quit the website if the judges requested it of me.

"If the judges felt it would be best for the court to cease your extracurricular pursuits with the website, would you be willing to do so?" Before I could respond, Rosenblatt interjected.

"Yes, she would," he said firmly. I nodded in agreement as Medgar continued to scribble furiously.

Just as Rosenblatt and I anticipated, Medgar upheld the outcome that Judge Levy desired. On September 8, 2005, I was officially fired from Lorain County Juvenile Court for purported violations of the court's policy, the range of which had widened exponentially since my suspension the previous month. Medgar's letter read like a legal brief as he threw in every possible handbook provision to justify my discharge, regardless of its applicability. Although unable to cite a provision that addressed the true source of his consternation, he invoked the classic "image" issue that accurately revealed the culprit: moral indignation. The notion that I "did not give the opinions of the Judges any thought or what their reaction would be to [my] appearance on a website in a partially dressed, sexually provocative manner" allegedly "demonstrate[d] a lack of regard to the image of the Court and perception of the public."

In other words, I should have known better. I should have conducted my extracurricular life in anticipation that "objective" judges would deem the Court's image to be hampered more by a bikini-clad magistrate than a repeated drunk driver. I should've bowed in anticipatory acquiescence to parents who teach juveniles that an intelligent woman who displays sexual appeal should not possess any authority. I should've shown more regard for the judges who stripped me of the credibility they claimed I didn't possess. Rosenblatt and I prepared for the appeal before Judge Beranski as I initiated an ill-fated claim for unemployment compensation.

Meanwhile, Jack and I awaited my final paycheck, along with the $10,000 I was owed for accumulated medical and vacation time. "So when are you going to get your medical and vacation check?" he asked. "This computer's moving so slow, the hard drive is fried. We should invest a thousand or so in a new one."

"They can't release it for at least forty-five days following my termination," I said. "It will be around the end of October."

"See? They're going to fuck you over. It will take forever for us to get a new computer. These website updates are going to get slower and slower."

Within days, Rosenblatt e-mailed a draft of his appellate brief. He covered all the bases. After invoking my First Amendment rights, he challenged the court's initial excuse for my suspension, i.e., that I failed to report part-time employment: "It is respectfully submitted that this is, and was, a subterfuge for dismissing her because some took moral affront to the nature of the photographs...." He took aim at the double standard by which Lugar assessed *genuine* income received from part-time employment practiced by other staff members, including those selling Avon, Mary Kay, and Longaberger baskets.

He also called into question Medgar's criticism of my failure to anticipate the judges' opinions: "This finding begs the issue before the Court and illustrates that Administrator Medgar had already concluded that Ms. Dean had violated the provisions of her employment prior to the hearing." In addition, he pointed out that the same personnel manual permitted me to be fired on a first-time infraction **only** for a "major violation," defined as "one that has a serious negative effect upon the operation of the court." The only evidence offered to this effect was Lugar's reference to "courthouse gossip" and the loss of "about two work hours" from numerous employees viewing the website on county computers. Rosenblatt wrote, "Ms. Dean cannot be properly disciplined for other employees shirking their duties to search the web."

His well-chosen words failed to convince Judge Beranski, who watched Rosenblatt and the county's attorney exchange several missiles as they debated the circumstances of my discharge. While my appeal was pending, Administrator Medgar issued a letter to my colleague Joanne requesting that she assume my old duties. Although she protested to Beranski himself that the move was inappropriate given the status of my appeal, Medgar's request was key evidence that I didn't enjoy the due process from the proceeding I dubbed a "kanagaroo court." The outcome was predetermined long before Lugar ever asked me, "Are you familiar with the V-Twin Girls?"

Following the denial of my appeal Rosenblatt researched the strength of a possible lawsuit, including the First Amendment issues that led him to consult with noted civil rights attorney Avery Friedman. He conveyed Friedman's concerns that the balancing test between expectations of judicial behavior and free speech might not tip in my favor, and my chances of winning a lawsuit on those grounds was iffy at best. After determining that the matter of public employees' free speech was unsettled in our judicial circuit, Rosenblatt informed me that I had a seventy percent chance of losing a case that was sure to be a precedent regardless of the outcome. The larger question, he explained, was whether I could face the emotional and financial ramifications of losing. His belief in my cause appeared genuine, and he offered to take my case on a quasi-contingency basis, provided that I front the money for depositions and other expenses. I took his assessment home, where I sought input from the most important person in my life.

"So he doesn't think you can win? Hate to say I told you so. I knew he couldn't do anything for you."

"These are simply my odds, based on his analysis. Your opinion is valuable to me, Jack, and I didn't want to give Rosenblatt my decision until we talked. On one hand, I think the court must be challenged. They want to starve me out without any dignity. No unemployment, no severance pay! But there's no prior cases that settle the issue in our judicial circuit, so I'd be swimming upstream. I'm not going to swim that hard if I don't have your support."

"Melissa, they're going to keep fucking you over. We're gonna spend more money on depositions and other bullshit. Besides, they can get into my background and I just can't afford for my military background to come out. I could go to jail for what I did!!!"

"True," I said, not realizing that it was hiss *lack* of a military background that might emerge.

"Again, all for what? Huh? For a seventy percent chance of losing and me going to jail?"

"Okay," I replied softly, "I'll call Rosenblatt tomorrow and tell him to settle with the court. They're willing to give me a neutral reference in exchange for my promise not to sue. That may be the best I can do."

"You think I'm right, don't you?" Jack scanned my face for validation.

"Jack, I'm proud of your military service," I said. "I'd never do anything to harm you or put you in jeopardy. I'll call Rosenblatt tomorrow and tell him our decision."

For me the choice was easy. Despite a queasy feeling in my stomach and a strong desire to call the court to task, I chose to protect my husband rather than challenge the cultural biases of the legal establishment. It wasn't until long after our split, and after passage of the statute of limitations, did I learn the true source of Jack's fear. As the prime architect of the V-Twin Girls' website, he would be a key witness in any civil lawsuit involving the group. Despite the lack of direct relevance his military fraud bore to my potential claim, the discovery process would inevitably weaken his credibility, for his phony heroism (especially in a post-9/11 world) could derail his testimony and cause me immeasurable embarrassment. As Benazir Bhutto once said, "I don't believe it happens unless God wants it to." It's possible that the universe didn't intend for me to challenge the court in its own arena. I accepted that as I closed a chapter on my life and accepted another loss.

9. NAVY BLUES

Be careful of what you do
Cause the lie becomes the truth.
- Michael Jackson, "Billie Jean"

Days before signing away my rights to the juvenile court, I received a welcome surprise. I was invited by a local community college to interview for an adjunct instructor position in their criminal justice program. Penny, the Rubenesque head of the school's education department, was impressed with my resume and the sample lecture I gave at my second interview.

"You're overqualified," she smiled, peering over her wide-rimmed glasses. "We have a few attorneys who teach here, but they do it because they enjoy it, not for the money."

"I've never been driven by money," I felt optimistic as I left my second interview.

"I'll give you a call within a few days," Penny said.

"So how did it go?" Jack asked later.

"Pretty well. I feel optimistic about it," I replied as I poured a glass of water.

"By the way, guess who got sued today?"

"Who?" I asked, frowning.

"Rod and Hog Heaven," he replied. "Several of his waitresses are suing for sexual harassment. It's all over the Canton Repository today."

"You're kidding!" I said. "Which ones?"

After naming a few, he said, "But that's not all. A few of the waitresses are saying some of the nasty stuff happened during that same night the V-Twin Girls hosted the bands from the 'Rock Never Stops' tour.'"

"You mean that night we hung out with them in Hog Heaven's party room?"

"That's the night!" Jack nodded. "And since I took pictures for our website that evening, Ron might need them."

"We don't know that yet," I said. "Let's wait. This case could be settled within a couple months. You never know with these things."

Days after our favorite Stark County restaurant was sued, I made my final trek to Lorain County's justice center, where I was scheduled to pick up my final checks from the court's administrative offices. The clerk said politely, "Okay, hold on just a moment. I'll let them know you're here." Moments later, I looked up to see none other than Kristy Hardnett-Robinson, the head of the court's fiscal department, striding down the hallway with an envelope. I came face to face with the diminutive blonde whose decision to press "send" threw Judge Levy into a tizzy. As she chattered about the envelope's contents, I stared at her with calm detachment as unspoken words flew through my head:

How does it feel to hand the final payout to the "Vanessa Williams" of juvenile court? Righteous indignation... it's a damned weird reaction for a girl who bared her naked ass for the camera at a probation officer's house party, don't ya think? What was up? Were you pissed that your motorcycle-loving husband happened upon our site and saw me in a two-piece? Did he say something that hurt your feelings? Whatever the true reason, it wasn't the moral outrage you claimed. Oh I'm sure you had the same look of shock you'd have if I tossed your tiny frame through that window right now. Fear not. Karma is a bitch, and she'll deliver a far more brutal ass-whooping than I'm capable.

Kristy opened the envelope to show me the two checks, and invited me to call the office with any questions.

"Thank you," I replied civilly. "Have a good one!" A good fall from your pedestal, that is.

Days after I retrieved those checks, Jack and I

were hit with several bits of financial news. Jack was notified that his former neurologist was suing him for unpaid medical bills, while I was hired as an adjunct instructor at Brown-Mackie College. The news of yet another lawsuit against Jack seemed to cancel out the positive energy accompanying my new position.

Despite his newest lawsuit, I began to enjoy my new professional niche in education. I enjoyed teaching the classes I was assigned, including juvenile justice, constitutional law, legal research, family law, business ethics, and basic computer skills. Not only did the job rescue Jack and me financially, but the college's stark contrast to the austere conservatism of juvenile court was a welcome relief that bode well for my involvement with the V-Twin Girls. Although I didn't promote our activities at work, the website was widely known among faculty and students, many of whom attended our events and signed up for our e-mail list. Save for a few female students, my extracurricular activities enjoyed widespread tolerance at the school. Finally it seemed I found a job that allowed me to express the intellect of Bhutto while camping it up Anna-style on my own time.

It might seem logical that Jack would relish my new employment, since it provided the financial cushion necessary for him to continue administrating the website and casting me in the role of Kitten. Yet it became another lightning rod for criticism when my evening classes conflicted with my availability to attend mid-week events or watch the kids while he attended a V-Twin Girl photo shoot. "That job is a pain in the ass!" he often declared. I initially protested his impulsive proclamations, but eventually learned to let his tirade run its course. Even so, he still attempted to engage or provoke me: "You know?" "Don't you agree?" "Great...you have nothing to say!"

I received even more flak when I attempted to

use our computer to prepare my lesson plans. For Jack, my request meant his website activities took a back seat for a few hours. Taking a back seat was something he couldn't handle well, as I found out. He heaved a big sigh before describing the importance of his work: "I have to put up more photos by tonight!" "I'm re-designing the Cool Rides page!" "Can't you see I'm in the middle of....?"

"Yes," I often replied, "but this job pays our mortgage."

"You're not even using your degree!" he growled.

"Yes I am, Jack. That just shows you don't know much about what I do."

"Fine," he said. "How long do you think you're gonna be?"

"Probably about an hour, hour and a half tops."

On the occasions Jack acceded to my request, I sat in front of the computer under his watchful eye. He entered our makeshift office every fifteen minutes to check my progress, often needling me with questions like, "Are you close to being done?"

When he wasn't feeling generous, Jack took one of two approaches. Either he encouraged me to prepare notes by hand or use the old computer that sat on the floor. Of these two options, I preferred to write my notes by hand. Using the old computer required me to move stacks of books and papers out of the way, and usually entailed continual interruptions for me to look up at Jack's monitor. "Hey check this out! Look at what I did to this page!"

"Jack, I'm trying to get my notes done here."

"Yeah, but you can look away for a few seconds!"

Obviously I preferred to sit on the sofa and handwrite my class notes while cats wandered nearby. Occasionally I paused to pet a furry friend that jumped on the sofa, only to be interrupted.

"You pet that cat more than you do me. I think

you love it more."

I looked up to see Jack in the doorway. "Don't be stupid," I said. "Besides, Sammie here is kind to me. He doesn't put me or my job down. He's happy to be near me. It makes sense I'd want to pet him."

"I don't put your job down!" he protested. "It just annoys me when you aren't available for weekday events, and when you have to put in time outside the classroom."

"When you add my lesson planning time with instruction time for two classes, it adds up to about a standard full-time job. Next month when I have two classes, I'll make about what I did at the court."

"Yeah, but you don't have health benefits," he responded, happy that he had at least one trump card against my job.

My lack of health benefits added a new twist to my ongoing battle with urinary tract infections. Within weeks of being hired at the college, I experienced the tell-tale signs of another UTI. I informed Jack.

"Oh great! What are we gonna do? We don't have any insurance."

"I'll call Planned Parenthood or some other clinic that takes uninsured people. I'll surely see someone." After several calls, I found an office that would take me the following morning.

At daybreak I drove to a free clinic in the seedy section of downtown Canton. I walked in the door and down the steps into the converted basement of a church. A woman swung open the top part of a divided door and held out her hand. "Hi. I'm Sarah. I have some forms for you."

"You don't have health insurance, is that right?"

"No," I said. "I just lost my job and began a new one. But I don't have any insurance at that place."

"That's okay, the only qualification for us to see

you is that you're uninsured. We're a non-profit free clinic with private funding, including the church. Now...what seems to be the problem today?" She looked at me with kind eyes.

I explained my maladjustment. Within an hour and a half, I saw a doctor, took a urinalysis, and was out the door with medication in hand. I was to begin taking both the anti-inflammatory and the antibiotic as soon as I got home. Jack later remarked that there were a lot of pills.

"Yeah, they didn't have a heavy duty antibiotic like the clinic I went to a few months ago. I have to take this for fourteen days, I think. Ah well," I shrugged, staring at the plastic baggie. "It's a free clinic."

"Well," Jack said authoritatively, "they should've given you a better one."

"I'm just grateful I have this much," I said, as I walked into the den to contemplate the coming holiday season. "So what d'ya wanna do for Thanksgiving?" I said. "Same thing as last year? Or do you wanna go to my parents' place?"

"I'll cook the same meal," he replied. "The kids usually come over, and the older boys will probably be in town, too."

Aromas of turkey and stuffing filled our dining room as my parents joined us for another holiday chock full of Jack's military mythology and tense laughter. As always, their visit seemed all too short. No sooner had we eaten dessert did we begin chattering about their departure. The following morning, also known as "Black Friday" in the retail industry, I was scheduled to work an eight-hour shift at a clothing store in Belden-Village Mall. Despite my holiday retail duties, Jack and I encouraged my parents to sleep in and depart at their leisure.

With coffee in hand, I walked outside into the wintry chill and started my car. Scarcely a quarter mile down the road from our house, my tires found the last icy patch that remained on the road. In a split second, I mowed down a mailbox ledge and found myself in a ditch as deep as my plummeting spirits. Without a cell phone, I had no way to call Jack. Thankfully a kind-hearted passerby picked me up and returned me to my driveway. As I walked in, Jack asked, "What happened?" I unloaded my brief explanation. He shook his head. "C'mon, I'll drive you to work." I looked at the clock nervously. There was barely enough time. I sat in abysmal silence as he railed about the three fender benders I'd had over the last year.

"That's it. I'm going to have to take you to work from now on. You just can't drive!"

After he dropped me off at the mall, Jack returned to find my parents disturbed at his assessment of my driving skill.

"I don't understand," my mom shook her head. "She's always been a good driver."

"Well, she hasn't been the past year!" he declared. "I told her to go up and let you guys know what happened. We didn't want you waking to an empty house. She came back to the kitchen, and was like, 'They didn't even come downstairs.'" I never said this, but I accepted the lie as a common practice for him: Shade the truth in order to drive a wedge between people. What better way to alienate my parents than to claim I was disappointed they didn't descend a few steps to comfort their daughter?

The tenor of my holiday season continued its steady decline. Despite the fact I was dependent upon Jack for transportation during the following month, I tried to find some joy in preparing for Christmas. We had most of my money from court still in reserve, but the fact I hadn't received a paycheck yet from the college limited our holiday spending. I used my employee discount for gifts, and did my best to see that my two young stepchildren were treated reasonably well by Santa. I asked Jack whether he wanted to help plan for the kids, but he assured me he trusted my judgment. Each time I alerted him to the status of my purchases, he shrugged it off. Finally the time arrived when I thought we should discuss our Christmas spending for each other.

"You know, I was thinking about the financial challenges we face this holiday. What would you think about putting a spending limit on ourselves?"

"Well," he sighed. "I just hate spending anything at all. It seems that's what Christmas is all about these days."

"It won't be 'about money' if we set a limit and stick to it. Lots of couples do it nowadays. Since we've got the kids' gifts nearly complete, I think we can budget about $80 to $100 for each of us. Does that sound like something you could live with?"

"I guess," he said.

"Well don't sound so excited," I said. "I'm trying to give ourselves some parameters so we have a decent holiday on a budget."

"But it's budget this, money that. I'm tired of it. I don't wanna spend anything this year."

"In a larger sense, any kind of spending hurts," I said. "But this is Christmas. From my perspective, when I shop for you, it's not the amount I spend that matters. It's the happy look I envision on your face when you open gifts."

"But why does giving have to mean money?" he asked.

"You're not hearing me. It doesn't mean money itself. It's the time and effort. For people in our circumstances, though, we need a budget."

"I'm just fucking tired of money crap!" he exclaimed with an anger that surprised me.

"Where's that coming from? Hey, look at it this way. At least we've...okay, at least *I've*... already budgeted the amount. I'm just glad we can afford anything for each other at all."

"I don't like feeling this pressure!" he yelled, his voice climbing. I hadn't seen this illogical outrage since the occasion of my first urinary tract infection.

"What pressure is exactly posed by this 'spending limit' topic? We have the same amount, so you're not pressured to impress me. I've done the planning, so you weren't pressured with that. Heck, I bought the kids' gifts, so you weren't pressured with that either. Help me understand, Jack, what 'pressure' you're talking about?" I asked as calmly as possible.

"And that's another thing!" he roared. "You shopped for the kids. I feel bad that it had to be done, and that I couldn't do it."

"It doesn't matter which one, or both, of us does it. It's done, Jack," I said. "So again, you had no pressure. And there's no pressure here, either- unless of course, you consider buying a Christmas gift for your wife to be pressure."

"Oh brother," Jack said, rolling his eyes. "There's the guilt trip."

"There's no guilt trip," I responded, as I became caught once again in his destructive conversational cycle. "It's my impression that you feel it's 'pressure' to buy something... anything... for me, regardless of the cost. Even if you have spending money in hand."

"But it shouldn't be about spending at all," he repeated. "Besides, I don't have a lot of time to shop."

"Look, we've pretty much proven it isn't about money. After all, you could go down the street to the Dollar Store and pick up a few cheap gifts. And you'll have time to shop. It seems you just feel it's not worth the trouble to get anything for your wife. It's like you don't wanna be bothered, regardless of how easy we make it for each other."

"Money," he grumbled.

"If you're determined to feel that way, I can't change it," I said, my eyes stinging with tears at the insult I was dealt. "At some point in the next week or so, I'll give you the money. If you want to use it, fine. If not, that's your choice. I'm just not looking forward to being embarrassed in front of my parents because you didn't want to take your $80 or so to Walmart down the street to get me something." Several groans, protests, and days later, Jack found it within himself to go shopping December 23 with the assistance of his eldest son Jack Jr.

In contrast to his approach on gifts, Jack took great pleasure in shopping for the Christmas meal, which entailed the most expensive brand-name ingredients that he could find. He inspected several packages excitedly as we walked down grocery aisles. After seeing him toss multiple packs of the same item in our cart, I was compelled to ask, "Do you think we need three bags?"

"Well," he said, "I usually use about one and a half. I want to get three just to be on the safe side."

"But hon," I said, "we've talked our tight budget this year. We can't do a lot of extras. I think we could save money by buying generic on some items, but name brand on the important things you cook with. Perhaps we should add up what we've got so far." I began to search for a pocket calculator in my purse.

"Fine!" he snapped. "If we can't even buy groceries, then what's the use?" He threw several items back on the shelf. "I won't cook anything this year, I guess." I stared at him, amazed at his all-or-nothing outburst.

"I can't believe this. You're behaving like a three year old, and why? Cause you can't have all the brands you want? You're aware, for instance, that we have four bottles of Karo syrup in our cupboard. We don't need to buy more. That could mean a extra stocking stuffers for the kids."

"I don't care. I'm just tired of this. We don't have money for this or that. When will it end?"

"Jack, grow up," I said, as my patience lessened. "I don't get everything I want either. It's called life. With some scaling down, you can still make the same dishes, and we'll have enough money to buy the ham from the Honeybaked store."

"Scale down," he snorted contemptuously. "Yeah, but you always seem to have the protein bars that *you* want. I'm trying to cook a holiday meal, here!"

"I don't always have the protein bars I want," I reminded him. "If I don't have enough money for them, I simply have cereal in the morning. Big deal. That's what's known as a budget."

"Whatever," he said as he stalked up the aisle in a huff. Like a mother with a petulant child, I walked behind him with the cart and placated him with a "deal" of sorts.

"Look," I said, "let's get what we need for the meal. I'm fine with getting these brands as long as you understand we can't do anything else for awhile."

"What else is new?" he asked indignantly as he loosened up and revisited the shelves.

Eventually the $140 worth of groceries found its way to our holiday table spread, which Jack composed with his usual culinary dexterity for the family. As he mixed gravy and prepared veggies with ease, I busied myself upstairs completing my toilette. Meanwhile, my mother tried to assist his frenetic creation as Dad stayed out of the fray in our den. He raced towards the table with a large dish in hand.

"Get out of the way," he said flatly as Mom

dodged his path. She didn't challenge the rudeness that was second nature to Jack, whose pace intensified as dinner time neared.

We feasted on ham, corn, potatoes, and other goodies as we chatted about a wide variety of topics. In keeping with holiday tradition, the good vibrations of family neared a speedy end. At one point, Mom and I found some quiet time in the front room. As we talked about the kids and various holiday traditions, I looked at our large Christmas pine and recalled the small table top tree that adorned my parents' Columbus duplex apartment during kindergarten. Although I nodded in acknowledgement as our conversation continued, I longed to pour out the thoughts that occupied my brain. I wanted to cry and blurt out that this was the worst holiday I had, but I was too embarrassed to explain why. In addition, I felt guilty at the prospect of saddling her with my distress. Unprepared to disclose our dysfunction, I continued our antiseptic exchange until the moment arrived for their departure.

Following Christmas, Jack's mood vacillated between morose and crabby as he diverted more energy and countless hours in front of the computer. He blamed his winter doldrums on a Christmastime combat mission that went awry years ago. Even though I freely accepted this military explanation for his self-described "depression," at times my patience gave out.

The week following Christmas, Jack and I stopped at Walmart for various household purchases, including toilet paper and water softener salt. After parking inside our garage, Jack divided up the grocery bags as I led the way through the door. "Hurry up!" he said impatiently.

"Hold on," I said, shifting the weight among the bags. "One of these is really bulky." At that moment I felt a thud on my back. I stumbled on the second step into the kitchen door, my right knee hitting the floor. I was incensed to find that it was no accident. "Why did you do that?" I demanded to know.

"I told you go get moving," Jack replied.

"That's no excuse for shoving me. How dare you disrespect me like that!"

"Oh c'mon! I didn't do it hard," he rationalized. "It just drives me crazy when you poke around. You move so slow all the time." He tossed a few bags on the counter and strode to the computer desk.

"I don't care. You never, *ever* shove me again!" After I put a few items away, I walked into our den and turned on the television. About half an hour later, Jack walked to the doorway.

"So, you still giving me the silent treatment?" he asked.

"I'm in no mood to talk. You're obviously not prepared to even acknowledge your disrespect. And without resolution, talking is unproductive."

"You're taking this way too seriously."

"Oh really, Jack? It's not the first time you've shoved me with impatience as an excuse. You did it to me in the Mexican restaurant last year. When the waiter beckoned us to our table, and I began to follow him, you decided to push me because I wasn't moving fast enough. And to top it off, when I called you on it, you diverted the discussion to the incident at Hog Heaven, like, 'Well you disrespected me too..you looked at that guy,' blah blah blah. If you had just admitted it then, perhaps you would've been more conscious about your behavior. But you didn't acknowledge it. And lo and behold, it happened again."

"Well I'm *sorry*! But you don't need to be such a cunt about it."

"Is that what I am just 'cause I call you on your behavior- a cunt? Good thing you didn't talk to me like that when we were dating. You were too smart to do that, weren't you?" Jack turned around and returned to his post in front of the computer screen.

Later that night he offered his version of an apology as we climbed into bed. For the hundredth time he alluded to his military history as he bemoaned his depression. "My shoulder's given out on me, my body's falling apart, and this is a rough time of year for me. I hope you understand."

"I can understand impatience; I just can't understand shoving me through a door and verbal abuse."

"Verbal abuse?" he said, raising his voice quizzically. "When did I verbally abuse you?"

"When you used the c-word towards your wife a few minutes ago," I said. "Calling me a name is a far cry from just being down in the dumps. Being cranky is one thing, but that's way out of line. What's worse, you don't even seem to remember it. And if you're not even conscious of it, that means it'll probably happen again."

"Oh so now I'm an abuser," he said. "Look Melissa, I'm sorry if I hurt you," he said half-heartedly. It was the farthest he was prepared to go in terms of an apology, a fact I had to acknowledge. He rolled over and went to sleep.

Not only did the New Year bring more temperamental swings from Jack, it also brought a Dell computer to our house and his fervent effort to protect the V-Twin Girl logo. Just as his respectful behavior towards me waned over months, Jack's initial enthusiasm with our electronic contraption eventually faded as his impatience grew during website updates. In the meantime, at his urging, I plunked down several hundred dollars of my remaining juvenile court funds and filed an application with the United States Patent and Trademark Office to protect our V-Twin Girls logo.

Suddenly my "useless" legal education became the reason Jack pushed for the application and business checking account should be in my name: "You're the attorney. You're better with money. You handle that stuff." Although I was unprepared to acknowledge it, this maneuver was unquestionably designed to protect himself from creditors, child support enforcement, and the Internal Revenue Service, all of whom were cheated out of funds he owed. It was at approximately this time mailings from the IRS grew more frequent, as the agency pressed my husband for the reason he didn't filed tax returns for 2000 and 2001. It was, he claimed, the fault of ex-wife Theresa, who allegedly broke her promise to file while he was overseas valiantly risking his life for the United States.

In the meantime, the V-Twin Girl team added new talent as Jack attempted to network with a local modeling agency. As we added ladies with experience in performance and cheerleading, our dance practices resumed under the tutelage of Gina, who choreographed most of our routines. This development eventually provided ammunition for Jack, who continually compared my look and performance skill with other team members.

His toxic comparative habit was particularly sharp with Brandy, a petite twenty-three year old former cheerleader with long brown hair and alluring dimples. She was also the subject of Jack's empathy, for her status as a military wife elevated her esteem in his eyes. Her involvement with the V-Twin Girls frequently served as a social outlet while she awaited her husband's return from overseas. If I heard, "You need to dress/act/dance like Brandy" once, I heard it a hundred times in the months that followed.

Although I smarted from the condescension of Jack's perpetual comparisons and critiques of my dancing, they were nothing compared to the disparagement he leveled against a facial feature over which I had little control. Despite being blessed with smooth skin and an absence of crow's feet, I had prominent indentations underneath my nose that showed up in photographs. Known by dermatologists as nasolabial folds or "smile lines," they were known as "scowl lines" in our house. Jack sighed in disgust as he edited my photos. "It's a snarl, more like a scowl. You need to be more conscious of your facial expressions!" he said. "You're gonna have to practice this stuff in a mirror...alright?"

"But it's more of a skin feature I can't help," I tried to explain.

"No it's not! It's not as bad in some of the shots. You just need to learn how to relax your face. That requires practice!"

"Or the absence of stress," I shot back.

"Look. Stress is in everyday life. You've gotta deal with it. When the camera's on, you have to hold yourself well," he instructed. "Don't roll your eyes. You don't take this seriously!"

"No," I said. "I just don't think you get the factors that affect the face." Whether it was genetics, age or a combination of both, I wasn't sure. But I was sure of one thing, and I later regretted vocalizing it. "Jack, the only way you change something like that is through injections."

"What do ya' mean, like botox?" he asked.

"No, that's for fine lines like crow's feet and forehead wrinkles. Collagen plumps lips and deep creases. That's the only way you change stuff like this. Posing in a mirror doesn't do it."

"Well, you've gotta get it!" he exclaimed.

"We don't have the money for injections. We're trying to save."

"This is our future," he said, pointing to the computer screen. "We need to find out how much it is."

I sighed as his pressure mounted. Like a river's buildup behind a dam, the rising waters of Jack's temper had consequences for our domestic environment. It was easier for me to acquiesce and release a bit of water pressure rather than risk a full-scale collapse. It was similar to the manner of his sexual overtures: pressure, plead, guilt, and more pressure (sometimes several times daily). If I wanted to sleep without being awakened with argument, I knew what I had to do. I needed sleep more than I needed a chemical-free face.

My price shopping for skin injections ended with restylane, an FDA-approved dermal filler whose safety and cost appeared superior to options like animal-based collagen. I made an appointment with the Western Reserve Center for Orofacial and Cosmetic Surgery in Canton, and wrote it on our calendar in a self-effacing humor that was now commonplace: "Melissa's scowl fixing appointment" was set for the following week. Days later I walked out of the office and paused in my rear view mirror to look at my reddened nasal area.

"Let's see," Jack said as I walked in the door. I removed the ice pack. "It's a little better; I don't see the lines as much," he remarked, scanning my face. "Probably hard to tell right now. How does it feel?"

"Numb," I said, struggling to conceal my disappointment at his lukewarm assessment. His mild approval was temporary, for his impatience continued during photo editing. "Your scowl's a lot better, but the lines are there. I still have to brush it out."

Numbness was the predominant theme for my face and my emotions. As my husband created a new and improved face with Adobe Photoshop software, I sat on the sofa petting Sammie, whose frail body reflected the fragility within my heart. I heard rustling and looked up to see Jack, who paused from his arduous task long enough to seize the television remote from my side. He shook his head as he changed the channel.

"That cat drives me nuts," he said in Sammie's direction.

"He's old and weak. I hate weakness."

His commentary was interrupted by the phone. It was Rod, our buddy. Jack paced back and forth with the phone receiver. After several "uh-huh" responses, he said, "Hey man, I don't mind giving you the photos. I'd just like to stay out of it, ya know?" Minutes later, I heard Jack sigh. "Alright," he said with resignation. "Just call me only if you think you'll need me for sure." He hung up the phone with ominous frustration.

"Great! It's all over," he said, his eyes wide with fear.

"What?" I asked

"Settlement negotiations fell through in that sexual harassment case. Rod's attorney is getting ready to send subpoenas to witnesses. Since I took some photographs that night the V-Twin Girls were there, we might be called."

"Alright," I shrugged. "We only have to testify to the truth. Nothing more, nothing less."

"You don't understand, Melissa!" His voiced raised in panic. "I can't get on the stand. Linda works part-time at a bar with one of the plaintiffs, and she's been running her mouth about this awful violent past I have in the military, and what a bad witness I'd make, blah blah blah. If I get up there, I'm ruined! Oh, god...."

"So Linda knows about the Nicaraguan incident?"

"Yes! And it's going to come out if I testify." With that, Jack ran into the hallway and swung open the bathroom door. I heard the unmistakable sounds of vomiting. I frowned in consternation over my husband's obvious distress. Although his nervousness at testifying was genuine, it was not the infamous "Nicaraguan incident" he feared would emerge. Rather he instinctively knew the fraud he'd perpetrated for so long would be revealed shortly. Without knowing the true source of his fear, I had no choice but to become a captive audience for his mournful self-induced drama.

"Oh god," he kept repeating. He paused again in the doorway. "What am I going to do, Melissa? They don't really need me if I just give them the photos, right?"

"Well," I explained, "since you're the photographer, they'd need you to authenticate the photos. That means the court would expect you to testify that you're the one who snapped the shots. Otherwise, the pictures can't be introduced into evidence."

"What if I suddenly can't find the photos?"

"It's too late. Everyone knows you took them, and you just told Rod you didn't want to testify. Wouldn't take much to prove that you destroyed or hid the photos. That's contempt of court."

"It's better than proving I committed murder!" he exclaimed. After twenty minutes of hand wringing, Jack came to a resolution. "The only thing I know of to do," he said, "is call in one of my last favors. I still have some contacts in the system. I might call my former admiral and ask him to expunge my record. I never thought I'd have to ask him."

"What do you mean- expunge your whole military record?"

"It's the only way," he said tearfully. "I don't even know if he'll be willing. People can do this usually if it's a matter of national or military security. But if he agrees, my military history is erased. Like it never happened. No pension, no VA benefits, nothing. I'll be considered an embarrassment to the Navy."

"Seems extreme," I said. "Do you think it's necessary?"

"I can't go to jail!" he shouted. "Thanks to that bitch Linda, I've got to erase my background. I know Rod wants these photos, but I ain't going to jail over this lawsuit."

"Do you still have a way of contacting your admiral?" I asked, unaware of how naïve I sounded.

Days later, I arrived home from work to find Jack in front of the computer, morose as ever. "I did it," he said. "I finally called him."

"When did you do that?"

"Earlier," he replied. "He's supposed to call me in a couple weeks to let me know for sure. This will take time, 'cause they've gotta erase my name from every government database. From here on out, I can't mention my military involvement." But mention it he did, for my husband's desire for false glory won out over his fear as he continued to brag to area residents about missions that never happened, comrades that never died in his arms, BUDS training that never occurred, and Purple Heart medals he never earned. Many evenings we left nightclubs and V-Twin Girl events, only for me to hear him say, "Gee, I shouldn't have said that, should I?"

The lawsuit against Rod and his restaurant was eventually resolved without calling Jack as a witness, but its ramifications had a ripple effect as Jack used the proceeding to explain an absence of military records in case anyone performed an investigation. Unfortunately for him, several people had already conducted an investigation prior to the ill-fated lawsuit, including my old buddy from juvenile court. It took another year for me to understand the results of his search.

In addition to providing a convenient explanation for missing records, the lawsuit also served up a double helping of self-pity that drove Jack into a deeper funk and gave him an excuse for more appalling behaviors at home. His world of phony heroism and self-indulgence was crashing around him, and he was taking me with it.

10. THE BEGINNING OF THE END

I make my way through this darkness.
I can't feel nothing but this chain that binds me.
Lost track of how far I've gone.. and how high I've climbed.
- Bruce Springsteen, "The Rising"

The "loss" of Jack's false claims to military bravery meant that he had to regain power somehow. The V-Twin Girls, and its so-called parent company JM Promotions, provided the perfect vehicle for his efforts. The diversion of his energy was made easier when the manager of his radio station "laid him off" from work. He delivered the news in a deadpan manner. "Yeah," he said thoughtfully, "she called me into her office and said I wasn't bringing in the sales numbers. Told me that I should spend the next year building up the V-Twin site. At least she'll let me have unemployment." He shrugged nonchalantly and made his way to the computer desk.

In the months following his mythically clandestine record expungement, his public bluster lessened but he continued clinging to heroism behind closed doors. Jack wrapped himself up in a box of Kleenex as he lay on our sofa and drowned his sorrows in homemade cheese dip and the military channel. He desperately wanted to identify with a bravery he didn't possess, and he was quick to cast aspersions on my empathy if I chose not to watch the barrage of military-themed material that graced our television screen. "Sit down and watch this with me," he often said with doe eyes. If exercise or lesson planning urgently beckoned, then I was flatly told, "Fine then!"

Months prior to Jack's military debacle, I concluded that I could rarely watch politically themed programming with my husband, whose philosophical righteousness blossomed into unabashed rigidity during our marriage. Save for the area of foreign policy, we had few political differences when we met, and even those variations were addressed respectfully. Suddenly the man who yearned to see "Fahrenheit 9/11" during our courtship and admitted that the truth lies somewhere between CNN and Fox News became a standard bearer for the right wing. Our discussions about abortion (especially parental notification) and the anti-war activism of Cindy Sheehan became full-fledged battles in which he appeared threatened by any philosophical deviation from his viewpoint. Moreover, his commentary on feminism and gender politics reflected a misogyny he never displayed during our courtship. "I know you're going to roll your eyes," he said several times, "but I don't care. Some women deserve to be raped."

Jack's dogmatic adherence to political machismo crept into his website administration as he tried to censor "Kitten's Korner," the column that served as my only intellectual outlet during the V-Twin Girls' existence. His attempts at control didn't stop with my physical appearance. Not only were several of my ideas shot down on the grounds that the subject matter would "alienate" our viewers, but Jack criticized my wording as "too intellectual" for our biker audience. "That sounds stupid!" he often said, as he edited my column before publishing it to the website. "You can't write that; it'll make people angry." It did no good for me to remind him that the biker community wasn't monolithic, for it fell on deaf ears.

"Besides," I said, "it's good for columnists to offer readers a devil's advocate position once in a while. Magazine writers do it all the time."

"But our audience doesn't visit the site to think," he said, as he tried to morph my column into a series of fluff pieces.

"If they navigate to Kitten's Korner, they're

interested in some kind of opinion piece," I countered. "You jazzed up the intro as if 'nobody's safe' from my opinions. If you don't mean to offer a tell-it-like-it-is forum, we shouldn't put it out there."

"Well, you gotta change this," he often declared.

"I don't gotta do nothing." My intellectual integrity was one area in which I refused to cede ground. "If you want it changed, do it yourself. But be honest and give yourself co-authorship credit on the page, 'cause they're your words, not mine."

"I'm not putting this on the site," he said one week after I'd spent several hours composing the column.

"Then don't," I said calmly.

"But we need an installment here! I can't leave it blank."

"Then I guess you have a choice to make, don't you? If you want to control it that bad, you could always write it yourself."

"But it's called 'Kitten's Korner,' not 'Jack's Korner.'"

"Exactly my point!"

"You know what?" he asked, as he threw a pen on the desk in frustration. "I'm tired of you acting like I control this or that. I don't try to control you; hell, I don't even care if men look at my wife in a bikini. I work day in and day out on this website, and I try to make it presentable."

"We can talk about your control another time, Jack; you're not prepared to hear it. But there's a difference between editing someone's writing for grammar or clarity, and controlling their ideas. You're doing the latter, so don't expect my cooperation. Do it yourself."

Then came his infamous mantra of self-pity. "But I do *everything*!"

"Oh please," I smirked. "You might have a career

in fiction writing." I had no clue how true my words were! I continued. "But in any event, you can take what I wrote or leave it. It's up to you." On this issue I refused to budge. Jack could pressure and guilt trip me into everything from restylane injections to diuretics, but I wouldn't permit him to manipulate my ideas. Even so, he inserted himself onto the page, adding his two cents worth alongside the words "Editor's note."

In addition, he used my literary voice as a cover for his political chest-beating on Biker Kitty's (i.e., my) fan page on the networking website Myspace. Although I didn't see it until much later, he posted a blog on April 14, 2006 under my name entitled, "Open Letter to Our Military and Warning to the Masses." It's long been my philosophy to support American servicepeople, regardless of my opinions on presidential foreign policy. But Jack's self-indulgent blog transcended troop support and entered the realm of macho rhetoric that didn't represent my perspective.

"This ...is about the survival of a nation that has the unfortunate habit of "white zoning". Military persons know what I mean. White zoning is the mental condition of walking around unaware of the surroundings. That is until a land mine or IED pops under your feet! Unfortunately some weak minded Americans fall prey to this very destructive condition and listen to the power grabbers in both the media and in politics! WAKE UP ...you LIVE in this country that gives you the right to dissent ... but a word of advice ... don't bitch about the soldiers, sailors, airmen and marines who lay their lives on the line everyday so you can protest them and make yourself feel better. I see an ever growing similarity to these protesters and power grabbers to those from the Vietnam era and guess what?? NOBODY WON THAT DEBATE NOBODY ... YOU DUMB ASSES! It was a national fiasco and we will never let those un-American

types do that to our young military people ever again ...
Simply...don't let this Kitten hear you dis our troops or this
Kitten will turn into a TIGER with nothing but teeth and
claws coming your way! Thanks again to the men &
women of our armed forces for your exceptional service
and damn you unpatriotic types who are only after
popularity or power."

References to "white zoners" (which
coincidentally included me, according to him), critique of
the "weak minded," railing against "un-American" and
"unpatriotic" folks... it was all classic Jack. During
countless political disagreements over the years, I'd
never referred to a fellow countryman (or countrywoman)
as "unpatriotic" or "un-American" simply for disagreeing
with me *or* the government. Rather, these were the
ramblings of a man who craved the same "popularity and
power" he despised in others. To accomplish this goal,
he co-opted not only the Navy SEAL experience, but also
my voice. It represented the same "weak mind" he
blasted in others.

Several weeks after his vociferous blog post, my
birthday came and went without a gift or flower from Jack,
whose attentions were focused on the V-Twin Girls'
preparation for Blossom Music Center's Barbeque and
Music Festival. Our team was slated to host a bike show
and issue a brief stage performance at the Memorial Day
event, which also fell on our anniversary. While the
occasion was acknowledged by Jack, its importance was
overshadowed by the team's responsibilities. Sweat
poured from his face as he walked to and fro in the
summer heat, pausing only for a swig of bottled water
and offers of assistance from worried faces. "Do you
need any help, man? You're gonna collapse."

One of our tent's male visitors was shocked to
learn of our anniversary. "You're kidding!" he exclaimed
as he turned to me. "He's a hard worker. You've got a

keeper here, hon." He patted Jack's back. "Happy anniversary, y'all!" he said before he walked away. I smiled silently.

The event itself was happier than our home, which was rife with tension as we prepared for our biggest gig yet, the North Coast Thunder Rally, also known as Ohio Bike Week. From judging a tattoo contest to hosting a bike show, the V-Twin Girls were a major presence at Ohio's biggest biker event. The week's festivities culminated with a rally in downtown Sandusky that included a stage performance by our team. Jack voiced worry that my sub-par dance skills would be on display for Ohio's biker community. "I'd prefer not to have you on stage, but we're getting paid for four girls, and we can't leave our team leader in Massillon. You're gonna have to practice!" Those words captured the atmosphere for the week, which thankfully ended on a positive note as we wrapped up our appearance and headed home.

Just before returning home, Jack raised the idea of filming a project in Lorain County. "I got a call today from Rennie Jones, that promoter from Cleveland that owns the country western bar. He was contacted by a manager of a fitness center in Lorain County. He might want the V-Twin Girls to do a commercial spot or something."

"What's the name of the gym?" I asked. "Could be really interesting to do a promotion in my old professional haunt."

"I dunno; he didn't say. Rennie's supposed to call me later this week if the manager's serious. He'll let us know."

The week's success faded as I returned to work and the unpredictability of my dysfunctional existence. One day before class, I took advantage of a few free moments. In an effort to figure out which gym Rennie Jones alluded to, I googled fitness centers in Lorain

County. Not many results popped up, but I was surprised at what emerged. As I scanned the site of one particular gym, I saw a recognizable face in one of the photos. It was Ed Bergman, my old acquaintance from the court's detention center. He served as a part-time trainer for the facility. I shot off an e-mail through the gym's website. "Howdy," I wrote. "Long time, no see. My husband Jack and I never saw you at JB's summer party last year. Hope all's going well at the court. Take care, Melissa." For reasons I didn't yet realize, it was a decision that nearly proved fatal.

Jack's self-induced tension reached a critical point one fateful June morning. As I gathered materials for morning classes and ensured that Jill got her cereal, Jack let Minnie outside as Poof and Sammie watched their canine friend curiously. Jill sat down with her cereal and watched the animal crew as her head bobbed to the musical theme for "Spongebob Squarepants." It was her last week of school. Suddenly Jack's voice pierced the air with rage as he saw Sammie squat right in front of him.

"Goddammit Sammie!" I looked up to see Jack holding Sammie by the scruff of the neck. "I'm tired of animals pooping in this house, especially one who does it right in front of me!"

"Jack," I started to say calmly, "he's old." Before I could complete my sentence, Jack issued another outburst when Sammie bit his hand.

"You fucker!" he screamed at the elderly feline. Jill covered her eyes instinctively. I saw Jack pound his hand into the back of Sammie's neck and throw him into the backyard like a rag doll. He stomped into the dining room where I stood, briefcase in hand. "I can't believe I just did that," he said as the ramification of his impulsive rage hit. "Get Jill in the dining to finish her cereal. I don't want her to watch Sammie out there."

I tried to normalize Jill's breakfast with small talk as Jack walked outside to Sammie, who lay in the grass. As she finished, I inched towards the back door and heard gurgling noises emanate from the motionless body. I turned away from the haunting sight immediately. My emotions went on auto-pilot as I tended to Jill, whose bus was scheduled to arrive shortly.

"Where's Sammie?" she asked.

"Your daddy went outside to find him," I lied. Moments before her bus rolled down the street, Jack stepped back inside. He felt the weight of my stare.

"What is it?" he asked. "Are you afraid I'm gonna do that to you or something?"

"Jack," I said with soft firmness, "we both know you need help."

"So you think I'm crazy?" he asked.

Instead of responding to his rhetorical diversion, I spirited nine-year-old Jill to her bus stop. Still in shock, I suppressed my feelings long enough to get through my class. Meanwhile Jack buried our pet in the back yard. The image and sounds of Sammie's death played over in my head for days. I wish I could've believed the same mythology we taught Jill, i.e., that Sammie ran away. But my head and heart knew the truth.

So did my subconscious. That night I was awakened by a loud bird outside our open window. I stared upward at the ceiling fan as I came awake. Suddenly I realized it was the distinctive hoot of an owl, my totem animal for almost ten years. Although revered by some ancient cultures and feared by others, the bird's keen night vision made it a popular symbol of clairvoyant wisdom, or "seeing through" darkness of all sorts. In 1998, I had an tattoo artist place the raptor on my right shoulder so that it could "watch my back" metaphorically. I tip-toed to our window to look for the source of the hoots, to no avail. I proceeded to the restroom and returned to bed shortly. Jack affirmed the following morning that our area was a popular stomping ground for several classes of the bird, including the barn owl, a breed long believed by Celtic tradition to hear the unspoken.

A week after the bird's ear-piercing wake-up call, Jack received another notice of financial bad news in the mail. He was being sued by the local dentist from whom he'd sought an emergency root canal months before. With no money to pay the bill of seven hundred nine dollars, the matter eventually resulted in a default judgment like so many other debts.

While Jack huffed and puffed about the dentist's suit, I prepared for what was to be my last solo motorcycle shoot. The long-awaited event came after what seemed like my extended hiatus from the camera. Even Jack remarked, "This is your first solo bike shoot in nearly a year. Better start taking your stuff. This has to turn out good." I took painstaking care with my appearance, as I consumed my diuretics and scheduled a hair appointment several hours prior to the shoot. I packed several bikini changes in my duffel bag as Jack and I headed to New Philadelphia, where the manager of the Red Onion Restaurant and Pub greeted us. I was received well by the packed house, who watched me pose before AJ, our young new photographer.

Despite the applause, my reception at home was anything but positive when Jack put AJ's photograph CD into our computer. Except for one compliment regarding my skin tone ("Those pills really made your skin look nice and tight."), I was the recipient of a verbal firing squad that found fault with everything from mosquito bites to dirt on my knees and hair that fell in my face.

"Couldn't you look out and see the hair falling in your face?!" he demanded.

"No. I figured AJ could tell through his lens if he

couldn't see my face."

"That's no excuse! You should be more conscious of your face and body. And what the hell is up with the dirt on your knees. Jesus Christ, Melissa!"

"That happened when I knelt on the ground in front of the bike," I explained. "I guess neither I nor AJ realized it."

"It's your responsibility," he said. "You know something? I can't use hardly any of these!"

Although I knew he was exaggerating, it would've accomplished little to remind him that he *rarely* used many photos from a shoot anyway. When he was frothed up in a dramatic tirade, he didn't want to be confused with facts. I let him run on about my useless performance. He paused long enough to notice my blank stare. "What, you don't have nothing to say? Answer me."

"I don't need to. You're going to say what you want, you're going to criticize what you want." I said calmly. I shook my head and continued. "You certainly don't behave the way you used to when I posed with the first bike."

"Well, the stakes are higher now. It's a business. You have to be much more careful."

"Careful? *You* need to be careful." I responded. "I didn't choose to make this a 'business;' it was your dream that I let you attempt to fulfill and use my name in the process. It's not going very far if you use the 'business' as an excuse to make me a verbal punching bag."

"Bullshit. I'm giving you constructive criticism. You said long ago that you could handle us working together in this, and now you can't even take it."

"This isn't constructive. If it was, you'd remind every other V-Twin Girl of their flaws. You don't have the guts to treat them the same way. No, Jack... when we started, you acted like it was a hobby that 'could turn into something' bigger. You set it up as a compliment to my beauty. You never announced, 'Honey, if we ever make this a business, I'm going to throw every profanity at your looks than I can think of.' If you'd been honest then, I would've refused to jump in front of the camera. Cause I don't need this."

"Oh, so you're giving up, is that it?"

"You heard me Jack," I sighed with resignation. "I just don't need the drama. Nothing more, nothing less."

While the photo shoots grated on my nerves and self-esteem, one bright spot arose the following month. On July 18, 2006 the V-Twin Girls arrived at Harley-Davidson of Cleveland to assist with a motorcycle giveaway and make a brief appearance on WTAM with conservative radio personality Mike Trivisonno. The "brief appearance" ended up being a three-hour exchange in which Trivisonno indulged in playful repartee with me and intern Allison. Although the purpose of my appearance was to promote our website and the Harley dealership, my on-air exchanges allowed me to flex verbal muscles that remained dormant during bikini shoots. In addition to being most fun I had during our group's existence, it produced a result that Jack couldn't denigrate. Due to Trivisonno's widespread appeal and listening area, our website's numbers shot through the roof. By the day's end my photo page alone garnered approximately half a million hits.

The positive feeling from our appearance faded as Jack's temperamental roller coaster worsened with each financial woe. From the breakdown of our clothes dryer to the termination of his unemployment benefits, I became the target of his rage when life didn't go his way. Against the backdrop of continual monetary loss, Jack also developed an obsession with my sexual history, inquiring often about acts that I performed with previous boyfriends. He exerted pressure on me to share the same activities with him. "You're never going to do that with me, are you?" he asked.

"Jack, everything's a matter of mood. There are some things I've only tried once or twice, and I prefer to leave it that way. Can't you accept that?" The true answer was no, of course. It was impossible for him to recognize that verbal abuse wasn't an aphrodisiac. He operated from the self-referential world of a small child whose desires were paramount. Despite the consideration and attention to my physical needs he displayed early in our relationship, it became non-existent. Like restylane injections, name-brand grocery items, and new cameras, sexual activity was no exception. Jack wanted what he wanted. Most importantly, he wanted to catch me in the same level of sexual deception he practiced. He went looking.

After I completed an evening class one Monday in mid-August, I stopped at Walmart to pick up some of Jack's preferred beef jerky. After rolling into our driveway, I stepped into the humidity, unprepared for what happened next. I dropped my briefcase in a chair and started to lay the Walmart bag on our counter. Jack appeared at the kitchen door, his face dark with anger.

"I don't think I can trust you anymore," he said, as he turned and walked into the living room. Taking his bait, I followed and asked what he was talking about. "Who is Ed?" he asked, sinking onto the sofa. I flipped through my mental rolodex, my stomach churning.

"I know several Ed's, hon. I work with two instructors at the college named Ed, one of my old colleagues at court is named Ed. I dated someone in high school named Ed, too. Which one do you mean?" He shot off the sofa, towering over me with his finger in my face.

"You know which one I mean!" he roared. I inched backward in anticipation of being hit. "Some of your e-mails to your boyfriend ended up in my spam folder tonight." He bombarded me with such surprise that I didn't even think to myself, *"Wait a minute, I wasn't on-line tonight."* His rage continued. "So, when are you and your buddy meeting for lunch, huh?"

"What? I'm not meeting anyone for lunch." I said defensively. Light dawned as I realized which Ed he meant. "I think I know who you mean."

"You sure *do* know! It's the same guy you have a crush on. You searched him out several months ago, didn't you?"

"Jack, there's no crush. Yes, I used to work near his department at court; we were on different shifts. And I didn't search *him* out; I searched his gym out. You remember when Rennie Jones was talking about filming the girls at a gym in Lorain County? Well, I started trying to find out where...."

"Oh shut up!" he interrupted. "You told me had a crush on you once; it's the same guy you mentioned while we were dating."

I sighed. "I suspect he might have back then, but he never did anything and neither did I. Trust me, we don't have that kind of energy between us! Once I saw his photo, I wanted to reconnect. I lost so many contacts from court, Jack," I said mournfully. "Except for JB, I rarely write or talk to anyone from my old job. It felt good."

"I bet it did!" Jack sneered. "I bet you opened up your e-mail everyday with anticipation. Even better, you searched him out on the college terminals, where you knew I couldn't get hold of computer forensic info. Admit it, you were planning a rendezvous with this clown."

"Of *course* I used the college computers. Think for a second. You've constantly got ours tied up with the website or dreaming up logos we can't use. I've gotta do my lesson plans there too. I check my e-mail at the college not 'cause I want to... but because I *have* to." I was aware of the kids' presence in the den, and became concerned they could hear Jack's tirade.

"Don't put this back on me!" he said. "You know what you were doing. Read this!" He handed me an e-mail printout in which I responded to Ed's inquiry about premarital counseling. He was considering popping the question to his girlfriend. He asked whether I went to premarital counseling, and if not, whether I wished I had. I wrote back that I wished I'd gone. Jack took this as a personal affront. "So you wish we'd gone to counseling before you'd married me, huh?"

"Yes. It would've been a great idea. Could've talked about issues like our blended family, which we didn't explore like we should've. We didn't address the kids' feelings. Sure, we talked about being a 'team' in terms of discipline but even that hasn't played out."

"So you're unhappy with being a step mom? Do you think this guy needed to know that?"

"You're twisting my words. I love the kids, but everyone would feel better if we had fleshed these issues out before going to Vegas. It's not being a stepmother that makes me unhappy, but the situation you put me in. It's like the V-Twin Girls... you set me up as a pseudo-authority figure, then undermine me. Discussing definitions of 'teamwork' in a counselor's office could've prevented that. As far as Ed goes, it was simple advice. He might become a step dad soon."

"I never undermine you to the kids! It's obvious you're unhappy. You told Ed that with different words. I feel betrayed that you told him our problems."

"You don't undermine me? Let's count the ways, shall we? There's the game you play by telling me, "Don't let Jill (or Jason) leave the room without eating all their dinner...," then you leave the room, and send them home with the perception that *I* made them do something.

You talk to me poorly in front of them, so why should they respect me? They're only kids; they learn from adults. No wonder they treat me like I'm not in the room, or that they seize the remote from my side while they *ask* you first. See, it might've helped if we talked in terms of specifics beforehand, not flowery generalized ideas of 'teamwork.' And don't bother to thank me for not telling Ed all this. The only thing I advised him was to seek premarital counseling."

"Why don't you just leave the house? If you're so unhappy with our family that you've got to e-mail strangers about it, then why don't you just go?"

"Is that what you'd like me to do?" I called his bluff. "Sure sounds like a copout. It's a lot easier to tell me to leave than it is to examine your behavior, isn't it?"

"Don't throw this back on me," he maintained.

"You said it, not me. Would you like me to leave, or would you like to address the underlying causes of what I said?"

"Listen. I don't mind working on things, but it doesn't mean you have to seek some guy out and tell him personal stuff. This is an emotional affair!" His voice rose as he pointed to his stack of printouts. "Oh sure, roll your eyes. But if I sent these e-mails anonymously to our friends and asked their opinion, what do you think they'd say? If they saw this guy write to you about lunch, do you think they'd believe you guys were up to no good?"

"Not if they saw my response," I replied.

"And what about your mom. What do you think she'd say if she saw them?"

"She'd probably wonder why you're in her daughter's e-mail," I said.

"You'll find out. You might as well know I've already sent the e-mail thread to her."

"*Your behavior will be obvious to her,*" I thought. He never sent the thread to my mother, but he was looking for an outraged reaction on my part. I avoided biting. "You know, Jack, you lunch with people of both genders. But me? I refuse invitations because of how insecure you are."

"Oh yeah, that's another thing. I saw you made a reference about how I 'might not understand' if you had lunch with him."

"You wouldn't. You've proven tonight that you don't understand."

"Well not when you go sneaking around without my knowledge! When were you going to tell me you were e-mailing this guy?"

"The same time I was gonna tell you about everybody else who e-mails me: not at all, unless it pertains to our activities. Answer me this, Jack. How can I 'sneak' and conduct an 'emotional affair' on an account that's open to you? We have each other's passwords. Think."

"I tell ya why you'd sneak. You'd conduct an affair because you're stupid." He lunged towards me again, and pointed his finger less than an inch from my nose. "You don't even keep control over your own e-mail. You better watch who you forward your e-mail to!"

"I didn't forward any e-mail to you," I frowned, inching backward. It would take two more months and my leaving him before he eventually admitted that he entered my e-mail account. But for now, he was on an accusatory roll that was taking sinister turns.

"I swear, if you guys ever have an affair, I'll kill you both! I've got the training to do it, too."

"So you're threatening our lives, Jack? Is that it?"

"I didn't say I'm definitely going to kill you; only if you guys cheat." I doubted that Perry Township police would consider this an "imminent" threat, but it sure felt imminent to me.

"If you're irrational enough to threaten, you'd see an 'affair' in anything." By the grace of God, at that moment Jason came into the den to let Jack know one of his favorite programs was on. I went upstairs to take my shower and paused before the gun cabinet. Nothing appeared amiss. Our marriage had come a long way from The Little White Wedding Chapel. Two years after my husband pledged to love, honor and cherish me, I stood by our bed verifying the contents of his gun cabinet to ensure my safety.

I wanted to collapse. I knew the madness had to end, but I didn't know how. I could demand Jack and I attend counseling. I could leave him. Or I could leave this life altogether. It was a morbidly quick way to end my pain. I pondered logistics. Jack's rifles were too bulky; I'd have to use one of his smaller guns. The horrendous thoughts that plagued my brain that evening were eventually vanquished when I realized that I couldn't put my family through the torture that would surely follow if I took my own life.

As I toweled myself dry, I heard Jack enter the bedroom. "I still can't believe what you did," he continued. "I've just got one more thing to say and then I'll drop it tonight. I know where that guy works, and I know he's on night shift. I've got a steel grenade with that fucker's name on it, Ed Bergman." It was a tactic designed to control me, but I took it seriously nevertheless. Jack truly knew where Ed worked, and I feared he could become a target for Jack's misplaced rage.

Once I climbed in bed, Jack reached for me. "I want to make love," he said. "Please understand. I love you with all my heart; that's why I'm pissed off." The thought of having sex made me want to puke, for my guts were churning with fear. What would happen if I said no? Would he interpret it as a sign that my desires are with

Ed, i.e., "A-ha! I knew it!" Would either of us become a target? I didn't know. But my body knew the searing pain as Jack accomplished his ministrations with unusual roughness, almost as if to punish me for his imagined betrayal. I cried out that "it hurts" when my skull banged against the headboard and he yanked my legs crudely, but the only response I heard was, "Hold on." After he rolled over, I went to the bathroom and wet a washcloth with warm water. It was easier to soothe my body's soreness than it was to soothe my mind, for the latter was awash with a tension that continued for the next month.

Tension remained in the air the following night, when the V-Twin Girls went to Youngstown to appear for a photo shoot to promote Diva Bikinis. The shoot occurred in tandem with a concert by the rock group Buck Cherry, whose promoters nixed the idea at the last minute. We moved our shoot to a different Youngstown venue. AJ photographed our crew as I applied the best phony smiles of my lifetime. The distraction provided by the event was only temporary. Jack's self-righteous lecture resumed on our way home.

"You better be glad that Buck Cherry fallout took up a lot of my attention tonight," he said. "I'm still upset, you know?" The missiles continued. "You're stupid. Do you know how much I worshipped you?"... "Do you feel like you did anything wrong?"... "You're on trust parole with me".. "You're going to have to earn that trust back, show dedication."

Jack's attitude worsened as the coming days brought more bad news. On September 1, 2006, a foreclosure was filed on our house for failure to pay real estate taxes, a matter that Jack claimed was the product of his absence in combat missions. "My old bankruptcy attorney says I could be eligible for a rollback because of being overseas during certain periods, but I never called the tax department." After receiving word of the foreclosure, his blasé perspective turned into indignant rage, "We have to find the money somehow. We just have to!"

To Jack, "find the money" was code for "find a person to bail me out." That role usually fell to his father, who accepted the onus of his son's debts despite the ogre-like picture Jack painted of him. His approach was consistent regardless of the obligation... real estate tax, federal income tax, the mortgage, child support, or buying Christmas gifts for his kids. Despite his lip service to the contrary, Jack attributed these responsibilities to others and prioritized them somewhere behind beer, sex and cable television. Like a happy-go-lucky infant, Jack was content to play with his toys (e.g., the computer, television, etc.) while others assumed the responsibility for his needs. Unbridled rage awaited anyone who reminded him of his obligations, as I learned when Child Support Enforcement Agency ordered him to seek work. Everyone except Jack himself was to blame: CSEA itself, his ex-wife ("Theresa is a fucking bitch; she wants to destroy me!"), the kids ("They don't love me"), and me ("You're the attorney; you should prevent this."). It didn't matter that my advice was ignored by Jack, who resisted the notion of obtaining a part-time job.

"It would give us some reliable income," I said. "You'd help me pay bills as our website grows, plus CSEA would automatically deduct support."

"I can't get a civilian job!" he moaned repeatedly. "I have to work on the website constantly! Photo editing, page updates...I wouldn't have time."

His excuses multiplied as I continued to bankroll his existence. He added gas lighting to his tactics one September day as I came home to find him pointing at the computer screen. The monitor sported an image of a semi-nude woman walking across the floor of a nightclub. In the small of her back was a grainy tattoo.

"I found this on-line. Where was this taken?"

"How the heck should I know? It's not even me." He pointed to the grainy tattoo.

"Oh, that's you babe. It must've been taken within the last few months. Were you at a club without me?" He speedily moved the mouse as I neared the screen. I protested that her shoes were blurry and her tattoo appeared fake.

"You *do* have shoes like that." Fifteen minutes later, his inquisition was interrupted by the phone. As he wandered into the living room, I plopped in front of the computer. Like most women, if there was one thing of which I was sure, it was the shoes in my inventory. When I clicked on the recycle bin, the unedited image of the mystery woman appeared: tattoo-free, shoes with a looped platform heel. When Jack hung up and re-entered the office, I pointed to the computer screen.

"Yeah, so? It's no big deal. I was gonna tell you eventually," he shrugged.

"No you weren't," I said. "You were gonna milk it for all it was worth." He rationalized his ruse by claiming that he wanted to use it on the V-Twin Girls' Myspace profile as a cellulite-free alternative to my posterior.

"It looked enough like you, but she had a better rear view. Hate to say it, but all your 'cheese' is back. I noticed that last night."

Days later, I discovered another on-line shenanigan when Jack directed me to the desk chair so that I could send a message on behalf of our website. Before I pressed "compose," I noticed there was an unread message from an adult website that welcomed him, complete with his user identification and password. Although he and I looked at "mature" sites together on a couple of prior occasions, he'd claimed he hadn't joined any in months. "It's dated yesterday, so you must've joined recently," I challenged.

"I didn't join. It's spam; I don't know why they sent it. You can delete it if you want." It didn't matter, for he undoubtedly retrieved the message from his trash folder later while I slept.

Jack's degradation was now as much a part of daily life as breathing. He barely contained himself one September evening while I placed a couple of V-Twin Girl posters for auction on Ebay. He hovered impatiently. "Stop chewing your gum like that. It's pissing me off!" Within seconds, he grabbed both sides of my jaw and squeezed to force my mouth open. In one movement, I smacked his hand away while simultaneously rising from the desk chair.

"You grab my mouth like that again and I'm gonna leave an imprint. How dare you? You've never treated me like you have over the last few months!"

In light of his worsening state, I was shocked when Jack came to me one night and proposed we attend an Akron-area festival celebrating Mabon, the pagan version of Thanksgiving. "I saw it on-line. It's this Saturday. You wanna go?" he asked. I didn't know whether he was trying to mollify me, but I happily accepted the chance to share the holiday with him. It wasn't without a price, for Jack hit me on the morning of the event with a demand that offended me: He insisted that I wear a V-Twin Girl tank top. When I protested that I didn't want to turn the observance into an advertising opportunity, he reverted to militaristic righteousness. "You gotta be on 24/7, like the military." I acquiesced, for I was grateful to attend.

The aroma of burning sage greeted me as Jack and I perused the outdoor booths. I assuaged my spiritual hunger by collecting catalogs and business cards in a frenzy. I didn't know when Jack would find an excuse to tear me away from the event, so I gathered everything in sight from this informational buffet.

Later that evening, Jack and I decided to visit a few area clubs. Our preparation was interrupted by Jack's frustrated efforts to locate a pair of jeans. "What did you do with them?" he demanded to know.

"Probably in the laundry," I said.

After I walked downstairs, I was amazed when he said, "You look beautiful."

"You're kidding!" I said, frowning in confusion. "I don't hear you say that very often. Just struck me by surprise."

"Well," he rationalized, "I don't want it to mean nothing."

Off we ventured into the night as we hit several area watering holes. At one point our conversation turned to the V-Twin Girls as we took stock of each team member's strengths and weaknesses. We agreed that Bella, our blonde realtor, had a great work ethic and a well-shaped derriere that captured our audience's attention. Jack discussed Brandy, whose dedication and physique I agreed were beyond compare.

"I admit, though, I'm a bit concerned about her," I said. With the way she starves herself in the day and parties at night, I don't know if she'll keep her figure for long." Jack's reaction was swift.

"Nobody can say a bad word about Brandy! I'd go to war for her!" he said emphatically.

"Where did that come from?" I asked. "I just expressed concern. I hope that for her sake, she keeps every asset she has. I just want her to be healthy."

Monday morning, I assembled the business cards I collected from the Mabon festival. I e-mailed the leader of a local pagan study group to request information. My excitement was cut short when Jack interrupted my evening shower.

"What's going on October 11?" he demanded. My guts churned with a nervousness that was all too familiar. Regaining my balance, I realized that he'd read my e-mail again.

"There's a pagan study group meeting that night."

"How do you know about it? What are you involved in that I don't know about?"

"Jack, you were with me as I was collecting business cards at the festival. We talked about me getting involved with local people. Remember?"

"I don't trust you anymore," he said, resurrecting the e-mail controversy with Ed. "You're either selfish or the most stupid bitch I ever met." His venom had no rhyme or reason, but he continued spewing it as I readied for bed. "Those people [pagans] won't do anything for you. It doesn't matter what stupid fucking cunt goddess or god, Gaia, whatever, you worship."

"You never really wanted me to make spiritual connections at Mabon, did you?" I asked.

"There *is* no god! That's the gospel," he declared, his anger increasing at my attempt to sleep without responding. "You *better* say something soon!" he demanded.

"Or what?" I asked. "I just want to sleep." His tirade wound down in about half an hour, but sleep didn't come easy to me. My looks weren't safe, my sexuality was vulnerable, even my intellect. Now he sought to control my spiritual pursuits with his insecurity. I knew that night that our married life was over as I knew it. Jack had already resisted my suggestion of counseling. I wasn't ready to use the word "separation." Before my consciousness would reach that point, I had to verbalize my experience and hear myself repeat the words of pain. There was only one person I trusted to hear it, and I couldn't call her around Jack.

The following evening during class break, I called Mom with an old phone card. I couldn't hit her with all my troubles in fifteen minutes, but my lukewarm response to

"How are you?" told her something was wrong. When she asked about Jack, my veiled references to his depression leaked the emotional tenor of our household. I bee-lined to the same office phone on successive breaks. Our talks continued intermittently during the next week. As I heard myself softly describe Sammie's death, the full ramification of my situation hit me. I anticipated a further downturn as Jack prepared for the V-Twin Girls' trip to the Myrtle Beach Fall Bike Rally. My inability to attend due to work was a sore point. Although my absence presented a lack of dedication to Jack, it presented an opportunity for re-dedication... to myself, that is.

Fearing Jack's instability, I planned to escape in secret. Although I knew he'd exploit the secrecy of my departure to the V-Twin Girls and family members, I couldn't afford to care what they thought. I was the one most intimately aware of our household dynamics, and knew what I had to do.

I inquired of fellow instructors about homeowners seeking to rent rooms. Renee, a long-haired English instructor in her twenties, told me that her landlord customarily rented rooms. Without divulging specifics, I explained why I was interested. "Oh god. I had no idea! I'll talk with Laura tonight," she said. Within days, I stole a midday hour to visit her house. A raven-haired round woman in her mid forties answered the door.

"It's not much, but you're welcome to stay with our dysfunctional family as long as you want," the self-described biker bitch said, motioning towards the yellow curtains in the vacant room. "It's a full bed; I've got a few linens if you need them. Renee rents the rec room; there's some space down there if you've got extra stuff like pots and pans." As we completed my tour, she asked, "Is $200 okay?"

"Yeah," I replied. It sure beat a $1400 mortgage

that ate up my paycheck! Laura nodded as I explained that I'd start bringing my belongings after Jack left for the trip.

I awaited his departure with baited breath. Our final days were filled with verbal bile, especially one Sunday when we returned from dance practice. "Your rhythm sucked. You didn't seem prepared. You looked like shit!" He turned his attention to my parents. "They didn't buy you dental braces, they didn't teach you how to ride a bicycle, didn't teach you music, nothing." Had they been responsible, he added, I might have a valid function. "You're like a China doll. Pretty, but useless."

His venom remained sharp right until the end. Since our business' debit card was in my name, we were forced to tell the rental place that I'd be the primary driver on the trip. I was concerned Jack might retaliate with automotive recklessness once he realized I was gone, but I couldn't let my fear stop me. "Hold on," I said, pausing to ensure I had the documentation.

"What did you do?!" he demanded.

"Just checking," I said. "Everything's okay." We kissed goodbye.

I sped home to begin packing. The following day I purchased a cell phone and began loading important numbers into its memory. Financial details also required advance planning. After initiating paperwork to remove my name from our joint account, I went to a different bank and opened my own. I swallowed my pride and revealed my situation to my supervisor, who instructed the front desk to screen my calls carefully. Male callers were to be informed that I was unavailable. I spent the next week taking my belongings to Laura's in progressive stages as I fielded late night calls from Jack, who verified each evening that I was home in bed. On the day before his scheduled return, I bid goodbye to the animals, posted a letter on the door by our home office, and left to Laura's.

Predictably, Jack called several people when he couldn't get hold of me.

"Maybe she went out with a friend," Mom told him, feigning ignorance.

"But the only friends she has here are mine," he replied.

"Do you know how unhealthy that sounds?" she asked.

Jack's searching continued until he called our friend Tammy, who left her residence in nearby Navarre to check our house. "The driveway's empty. I don't see her, Jack," she told him, holding her cell phone as she was greeted by Minnie inside the empty building. She saw the envelope taped to the office door and stopped. At his request Tammy read the letter's contents.

"Just stop," he said. He collapsed in the arms of several V-Twin Girls, who assisted him to the rental car and valiantly tried to dry his eyes with tea and sympathy. None of them could imagine the relief I felt as I sat on the rickety bed and stared at waist-high boxes that lined my small bedroom. I was at a temporary loss as I tried to figure out how to fill the void of time previously occupied by the business and Jack's continual drama. Then it occurred to me. I turned on the CD's that *I* liked, read the books that *I* enjoyed, and did the lesson planning that *I* needed. In the days that followed, I crept around Laura's house like a cautious cat gingerly exploring new surroundings. I found myself apologizing for things that Jack normally abhorred, like leaving an item on the counter top.

"Shit, girl," Laura said, waving a carefree hand as a cigarette dangled from her lips. "Don't worry about it."

I spent my first free weekend settling into Laura's, but I couldn't wait to come home the following Friday. It was the weekend of Universal Light Expo, a Columbus area metaphysical fair that my parents had introduced me to years prior. My homecoming couldn't have occurred at a more spiritually appropriate time.

I hopped into my car. Thanks to Rock 107, Ozzy Osbourne serenaded my sojourn on Interstate 77 in a slow haunting melody that seemed coincidental. *"Times have changed, and times are strange. Here I come, but I ain't the same. Mama I'm coming home."* Times had changed, and I certainly wasn't the same. But perhaps it was for the better. My spirits soared as I glanced at the midday sun, whose rays were a bonus. I didn't care about the sunshine, but as Ozzy growled, *"I'm coming home."*

EPILOGUE

It's been too long, my spirit's been at war.
Havasupai shaman, let me be reborn.
And I will embrace the sun upon my face
Come the day I awake the child inside.
- Martin Page, "In the House of Stone and Light"

A month following my departure Jack and I began discussing reconciliation. Like many women in abusive relationships, I accepted his willingness to participate in marital counseling as a sign of his intention to change. The imminent foreclosure on our house added a wrinkle to our reconciliation, so Jack and I began scouting affordable apartments. Within weeks we cemented our reunion by moving into a two bedroom apartment down the street from our old house.

For three and a half months, I watched him slowly take over counseling sessions with phony apologies as he continually blamed his behavior on depression over his lame shoulder and the loss of a non-existent military background. Despite the fact our counselor purportedly had experience dealing with couples with a history of abuse, the well-intentioned gentleman permitted Jack to dominate sessions in the same manner he attempted to control discussions at home. Without the rigorous honesty and dedication required for true change, the outcome was predictable.

Our honeymoon period faded as Jack gradually reverted to old behaviors, often resorting to tantrums that increased in severity and frequency. Jack had to sign over his old house, I was laid off from the college, and agencies like the IRS and Child Support Enforcement Agency were knocking at his door. I watched his responses to these stressors in order to gauge his progress.

Sexual coercion also reared its ugly head again, resulting in an exceptionally bad incident in which he attempted to perform an unwanted act and stood over my naked body screaming at my inability to accommodate his expectations. Despite Jack's return to his brutish tactics, I remained confident in my ability to leave if necessary. I did it before, and I knew I could do it again. "It's a matter of time," I informed my mother as we spoke on the phone one wintry night.

The final blow happened one day following Valentine's Day. Upon receiving word that his driver license was suspended by CSEA, Jack flew into a rage, blaming me for not rescuing him. When he threw his glasses across the kitchen, called me a cunt, and threatened suicide, my course of action was clear. Patience be damned, I was not going to be a verbal punching bag any longer.

As our television blasted wall-to-wall coverage of Anna Nicole Smith's death, I secretly gathered basic clothing and supplies in garbage bags and spirited them to my car. When I arrived at my gym the next day, I made a few calls. The first was to my old friend from juvenile court, JC.

"Listen," he said flatly. "You've gotta get away from that guy."

"I'm two steps ahead of you. You know any homeowner around there that's renting rooms or apartments?"

Then I called Mom. "Just come on," she said. On February 16, 2007 I left and didn't look back.

Jack subsequently took steps to win back my affections. In addition to increasing the frequency of his private counseling sessions, he secured a full-time retail position that permitted automatic child support deductions from his paycheck. He quit the position a few months later, opting for the allure of cash income he earned from bouncing in local bars.

On June 28, 2007 the Stark County Domestic Relations Court granted our dissolution and eliminated my hyphenated moniker: "Wife is restored to her former name of Melissa Dean." My identity no longer split, I set about to the task of restoring all aspects of my identity and integrating the appeal of Anna Nicole with Bhutto-esque advocacy.

I reconnected with old friends, constructed my own Myspace profile, scheduled my own photo shoots, and rebuilt my life. When he saw new photos of me on-line, Jack immediately called the former shutterbug for the V-Twin Girls and demanded to know why he snapped photos of a woman whose image still "belonged" to him. He pumped the lad for information on my dating life and current address, which I kept private for obvious reasons. (In August he followed up his queries with an on-line search for my address.)

My journey was enlightened by revelations that arrived two months following our divorce. As I reconnected with old friends, JC clarified the military research results that escaped my consciousness in 2004. "No, hon, I didn't say Jack served admirably," the Navy veteran said one August evening. "I said we found nothing on him, and he *could have* served in a private contracting capacity. But I don't think he did that either." This was confirmed by independent research conducted in 2004 by a mutual acquaintance of Jack and me. Despite the unmitigated fraud perpetrated in our sessions and the community, my ex-husband clung to this fantasy after our divorce, referring to himself in a Myspace blog as an "old salt"[6] with "twenty years of hyper-military training."[7]

After quitting his retail position, Jack was evicted from the apartment we shared. Upon hearing of his impending removal, my immediate concern was for our cat Poof, who I feared would become a victim of his instability. I removed the e-mail block on Jack long enough to ask, "Are you moving to an apartment that accepts cats?" Despite the stilted tone of our electronic exchange, we arranged a transfer for the animal. With the help of a close friend, I drove to Massillon and rescued the furry being that has served as my companion ever since. I quickly reinstituted the e-mail block.

Since both our names were on the lease, Jack's eviction left yet another black mark on a credit rating I'd worked hard to rebuild. Despite being unable to afford the rent, he purchased the shiny Harley motorcycle of his dreams, only to have it repossessed months following his eviction.

When a couple of his ex-girlfriends sought me out for support in the fall of 2007, I confided my experience to them, after which I received a righteous declaration: "..for you to label me as an abuser is beyond reproach. I have no idea why you would take this route. Yes I freely admit I made huge mistakes in our marriage. I own them.... Please for my own mind what makes you think I am what you claim?"[8] True to form, Jack never fessed up to the deception, manipulation, and abuse that he claimed to "own." I came to terms with the fact that I would never hear any admission on his part. Instead, I had to focus on my own development.

My efforts to reclaim myself were aided by tender love from a source that I never expected. After twelve years of platonic friendship, in September I began to date the brother of a dear friend. As my comfort grew we looked at each other through a newly discovered romantic lens through which I saw trust, respect, and dedication. We are now engaged to be married. In an amusing side note, Jack subsequently circulated an allegation in his community that I'm engaged to the man with whom I was "cheating" while married to him. I shook my head, laughing at his latest concoction.

Last year, I began to pen a work describing my experiences. During its creation, I participated in a photo shoot with Cleveland photographer Gregoire McElrath, whose innovation captured the duality of my Anna-Benazir spectrum. It was my goal to use a few of the shots in conjunction with my new work, which I looked forward to sharing at its spiritual birthplace: the 2008 Universal Light Expo. I enthusiastically made the transition from attendee to vendor and submitted an ad for the event program. Like several vendors and presenters, I included a photograph of myself in my ad. It was McElrath's shot featuring me lounging in a business suit of white, the color of purity and healing. I was saddened to learn the ad was rejected by event organizers, one of whom e-mailed a polite characterization of my photo as a "pinup." Despite my disappointment, I dutifully submitted a second ad that I hoped wouldn't offend anyone.

I took a long hard look at the woman in the photograph. She was a woman of physical appeal that transcended cheesecake. Makeup highlighted her appeal, but didn't overshadow it. Her white business suit was far more modest than a bikini, but it wasn't asexually shy. Her direct gaze was strong without being come-hither, and her leisurely pose was confident. At any moment, this suited lass could smile, frown, blow a kiss a la Anna Nicole, or rise to her feet and deliver a closing argument. Or she could quietly remain seated in the awkward center of a spectrum of beauty and intellect, calmly observing efforts to place her in categories imposed by others: an exploitative husband, a conservative court system, and even well-intentioned liberals. She could take a path of her own choosing. She could simply be herself.

Photo: Gregoire McElrath

[1] "Musharraf: Bhutto To Blame For Her Assassination," CNN.com, January 6, 2008.

[2] "Drugs That Killed Anna Rx'd To Howard K, Others," TMZ.com, March 31st, 2007.

[3] "Geraldo At Large," Fox News network, October 20, 2007.

[4] "Living and Dying in the Spotlight," *The Seattle Times,* February 9, 2007.

[5] "Tape: 'She's Not Breathing, It's Anna Nicole'," *The Miami Herald,* February 13, 2007.

[6] Myspace Blog, myspace.com/snitesbobber, July 24, 2007.

[7] Myspace Blog, myspace.com/snitesbobber, August 23, 2007.

[8] Myspace message, October 8, 2007, 12:59:00.